THORNABY STORIES
Features from Thornaby Pride Magazine

DEREK SMITH

Published by Thornaby Town Council

Thornaby Pride

The articles in this book were published over the last three years in Thornaby Pride magazine. With the decline of local print journalism this community voice has grown more important to the town of Thornaby. Now the Council has also helped to create a proper archive where material like the photographs and stories contained in this book can be preserved for future generations.

Thanks to Dr Julia Routh and her colleague Sarah Booth there is now a hub for Thornaby photographs, memorabilia and stories to be archived and it is growing by the week. Julia encountered the important Remembering Thornaby Collection in 2021, the files were being stored at the Town Hall for safe keeping after the group disbanded and she realised the value in restoring them. Thanks to her goodwill and the support of Thornaby Town Council the archive is now developing, is accessible and receiving the professional attention it deserves. Local volunteers like John Watton, Craig Willis and David Thompson have joined to create a team at the Town Hall to handle the remarkable collections that include the Aerodrome and the Civic collection of the Council as well as the extensive Head Wrightson Collection.

Thornaby Council Archives
John Watton, Sarah Booth, Dr. Julia Routh and David Thompson.

Julia Routh talks to Head Wrightson worker Don Lackenby in the Archive's tent at Thornaby Show.

A couple view an Archives display during Warm Welcome day.

Recent additions to the archive:
From top: Winifred Hope's manuscripts. (See pages 89-96)

Jimmy Dank's Far East diary and photographs. (See pages 103-107)

Bon Lea Foundry album, donated by Anne Irish.

When our **Thornaby Lives** book researched the creation of Thornaby in 1892 we could find no image of Charter Day, a key event in the Town's history when the streets of Thornaby were thronged with rejoicing citizens. Recently Morwenn Breare contacted us with a beautifully preserved album of Victorian snapshots which she tells us was nearly destroyed when her grandmother who had inherited it died. At last we now have this remarkable photograph of that historic day taken from the flat above Fiddlers the butchers overlooking the Five Lamps and Mandale Road. Note the plot of vacant land to the left of the flag on the right, soon the Market Hall would be built here and later in 1913 converted to Thornaby's first cinema, the Edisonia Picture Palace which became the much loved Queen's .

The Album was a birthday gift to Morwenn's great grandmother J.B. Brenkley in 1896
and it is possible that the girl on the right is her, she is with Captain Salt's Number 3 Battery of North York Artillery and it's impressive horses and carriage seen in the earlier procession

Census Treasure

Pottery Street 1911, this remarkable photograph preserved by Raymond Todd captures some of his family. Who were they are what happened to them? Fortunately in 1911 there was a Census taken which helps us to piece together this fascinating story.

Census research reveals the Staffordshire roots of many of the Pottery Street residents and confirms the story of Stockton's William Smith who established the factory in 1824 recruiting skilled workers from the potteries. Pottery Street was built to house them.

Ray's own family story and the Thornaby connections start in Pottery Street one of the earliest Streets to be built in Thornaby. In fact two strands of Ray's family began their Thornaby lives in this street with on his mam's side Thomas Ions from Seaton Sluice/ Hartley at number 59 and further up the bank Robert Heslop from Millwall, London at number 20. They lived here at about same time. Did they know each other, were they friends? We can only guess.

What is certain is that before leaving for Thornaby Thomas Ions partner Hagar Durrant together with sisters Mary, Elizabeth and their mother all from Burnham Overy in Norfolk had ended up in the Seaton Sluice /Hartley area in the 1860's. Sisters Mary and Elizabeth would go on to marry the same man: Robert Brown. Firstly Elizabeth who appears to have died in the 1870's then Mary who moved from Seaton Sluice with husband Robert to 1 Stanley Grove in Thornaby where we find them in the 1881 Census.

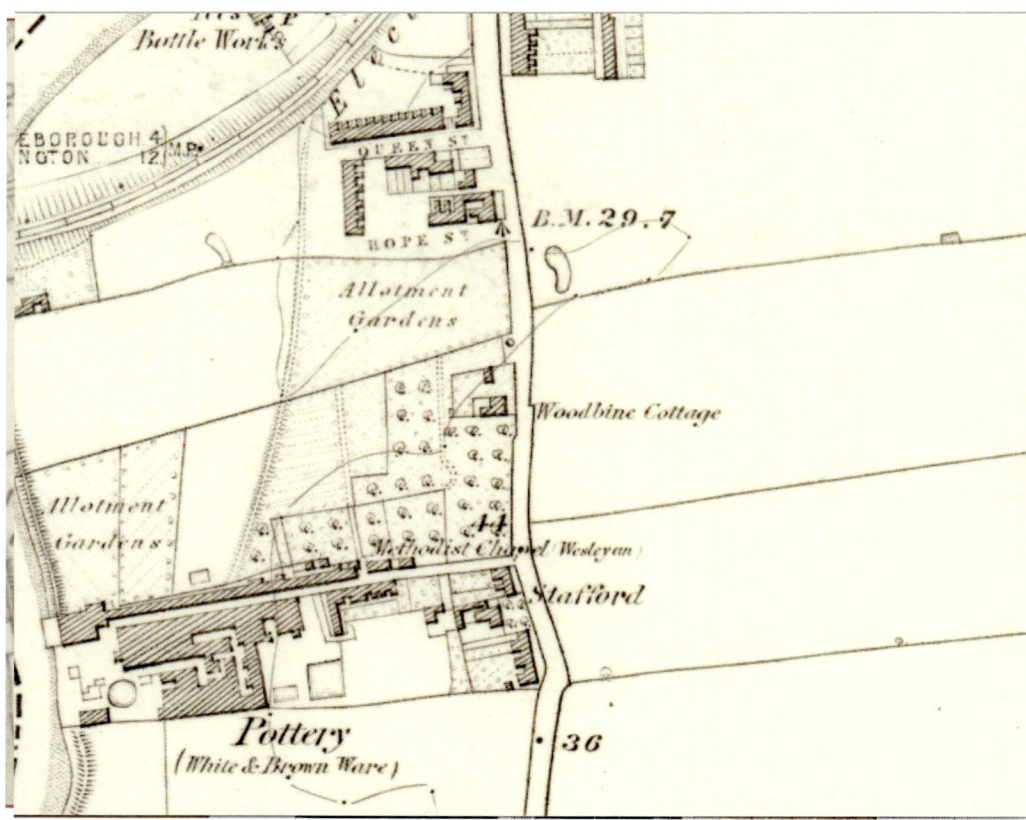

By 1856 few dwellings had been built around Stafford Pottery even though production began as early as 1824 making brown ware. Nearly 100 people worked on the riverside factory and many may have encountered long journeys to get to work. A small community developed around Queen Street West seen at the top of this map. Before industry and human waste took their toll on the river residents of these cottages fished for salmon in the nearby Tees which is out of frame on the left.

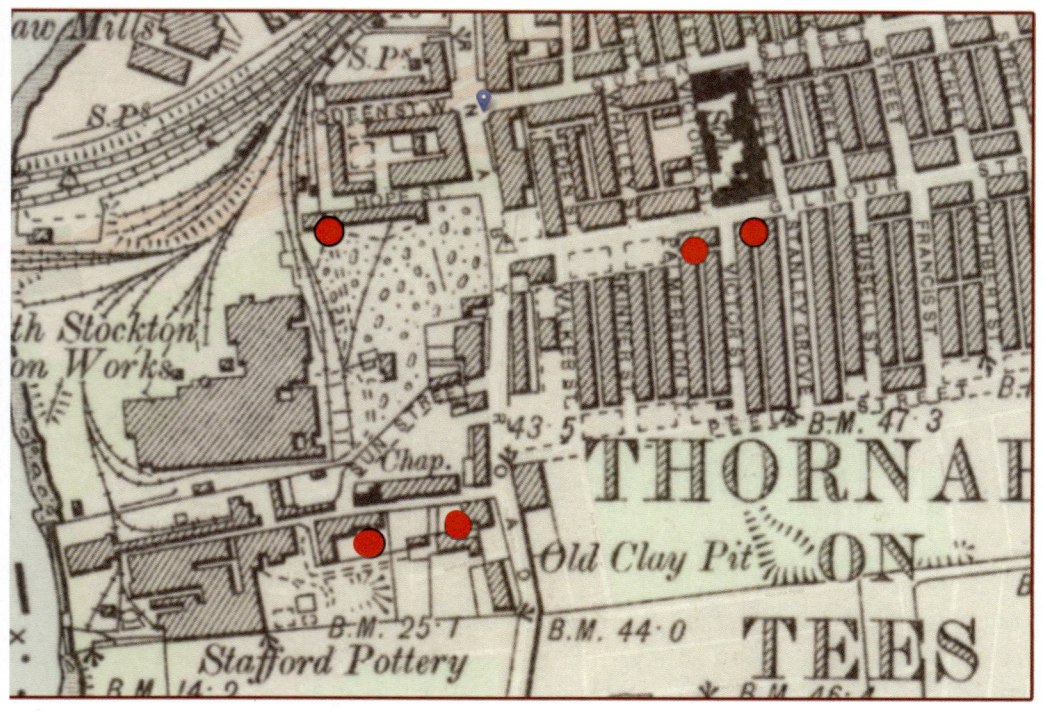

Thornaby's remarkable expansion is revealed in this 1896 map. The red dots mark Ray's family residences in Pottery Street, Hope Street. Stanley Grove and Gilmour Street.

It is fanciful to imagine a frontier spirit emerging in the new town when residents arrived from all over Britain in search of a better life.

In the 1911 photo:

Annabella Heslop 1895-1943 holds her sister Sarah Heslop b.1910

Mary Tighe b.1887 was also recently identified in the group photograph. She holds her daughter Mary Ann they lived at 16 Pottery Street.

Ray's great great grandfather Robert Thomas Heslop 1864-1937 a shipyard riveter from Millwall, seen in "The Rec." in about 1930.

Annabella Broderick, Ray's great great grandmother b.1838 lived at number 29 Pottery Street. her partner Matthew a pottery kilnsman was 73 at this time. When Stafford Pottery folded he appears to have found work in the corporation depot. Matthew went missing on a works outing to South Shields on July 7th 1913, his body was found in the River Wear two days later, the tragic incident remains a mystery

Bottom left, Ray's grandmother Ruth with brother Matthew Heslop. Ruth moved down the hill to Hope Street to marry Fred Todd in 1926 seen on the right outside their home.

Below right, a world away from their early roots and it appears none the worse for the experience: three Heslop sisters Jenny, Sarah and Ray's nana Ruth, first right, with a friend Clara (Left) in Jenny's Trafalgar Street shop, McKewans during the mid 1950's.

A Family Home: 46 Gilmour Street

The many stories of a family house: "I was born in the front room of this home in 1951" Ray tells us. One of four built on Stanley Grove by John Roper in 1873. The gable end view of the family home for fifty years looks elegant, in fact Stanley grove houses were also poky two up two downs. The only street in old Thornaby to have gardens Stanley Grove was even considered posh but it seems available living space was sacrificed as a result.

What subsequently develops around three neighbouring houses in a very small area of Thornaby demonstrates the nature of extended family life in the old town. Robert Brown disappears from Stanley Grove and a niece Elizabeth Ann the daughter of Thomas and Hager Ions from Seaton Sluice/ Hartley moves in with Mary Ann Brown joined by her partner Ralph Higginbotham a local man and their family of six including Ray's grandmother Hagar. Ten years later the family have moved next door to 46 Gilmour Street, but the intervening years have brought tragedy.
By 1911 the Higginbothams have lost two children at the ages of three and five: Ellen and Catherine who both died in 1904; Elizabeth Ann also loses her aunt Mary Brown (Durrant). Another of the original Durrant sisters Hager Ions joins them at 46 Gilmour Street but without her husband Thomas Ions. The Ions family had lived across the road at 50A Gilmour Street with their children after moving from Pottery Street. So the Durrant sisters provide the continuity and the links between families and homes and it is likely the Ions moved to 50A Gilmour Street to be near Stanley Grove and their relatives.

Cramped dwellings like Stanley Grove where up to eight people in the Ions and Higginbotham families lived in four tiny rooms became havens for contagious diseases, a decade earlier the area had been recorded as a fever hotspot. Hager Higginbotham's two daughters were possibly lost to diphtheria.

A section of the plans passed by South Stockton local board to build 46 Gilmour Street and 1, 3, and 5 Stanley Grove in 1873. Ray's relatives' two houses are on the right hand side of this drawing which shows their narrow design.

Ray's great grandmother Elizabeth Ann Higginbotham 1871-1951 walking back to Thornaby from Stockton in about 1930. On the right, the Empire Theatre and the gates to the Castle Brewery. Elizabeth lost two of her six children in 1904 but remained positive about life, she died at 46 Gilmour Street in 1951 a few months before Ray Todd was born in the same room.

Mystery still surrounds some of our Census discoveries, for example why was Hager Ions recorded as a widow in Gilmour Street 1911 when Thomas Ions did not die for another ten years until 1921 after returning to his roots at Seaton Sluice with Hager? Both ended their days together on idyllic Rocky Island at Seaton Sluice, Hager died in 1929 aged 85 leaving £454, a small fortune then.

Above: Thomas and Hager Ions. Born in Hartley in 1841 Thomas would have witnessed the aftermath of the 1862 pit disaster when 205 men were killed. Understandably many parents were eager for their children not to go down the pit. The lure of emerging industries in Thornaby may have attracted Thomas who was the Stafford Pottery engineer for a while. Hager's father John Durrant a master mariner from Norfolk is living with them in the 1871 Census at Pottery Place working as a labourer. John must have decided to stay, we find him in Lucan Street Stockton in 1881 aged 71 with Mary his partner, Hager's mother.

The Census

Let us celebrate the Census enumerators of yesterday who tramped the streets
Persuading residents to complete these essential records. Not only are they a
Guide to the public services we need but they tell us who we are at a given
Moment in history. Without them our family trees would be impossible to piece together.

Our thanks to Raymond Todd for sharing his photographs and family stories.

The 1921 Census

A tally of households in the UK has been made every ten years since 1841 but 1921 is a key year because we had to wait another 30 years until 1951 before any more Census details were recorded. Why the long gap? Well tragically the completed 1931 census was mysteriously destroyed by a fire in 1942 and to compound this no proper Census was taken in 1941 because of the war. We looked at two Thornaby families in the 1921 Census and invited some of their descendants to help us discover what happened to their families in the following years.

Above: Belsen, a demented camp prisoner, April 1945. James Payne was part of the group that liberated Belsen Concentration camp.

1. James Alfred Payne 13 Britannia Street

When James Payne's father filled in the Census form for his son in 1921 could he ever have imagined the apprentice boat builder would go on to witness the horrors of the holocaust? Jimmy rarely talked about his momentous war years and earlier but just before his death he revealed some of the story to son Ken:

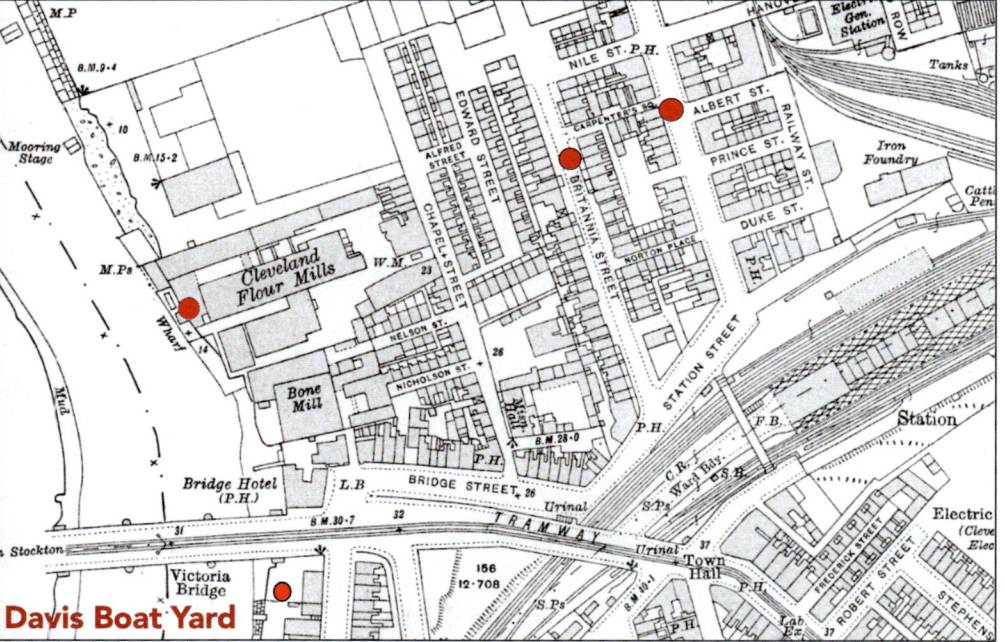

Davis Boat Yard

The parochial nature of Jimmy's early years is shown in this 1915 map of Thornaby's main industrial area, " Below the Railway" He was born in Carpenter's Square, then the Paynes moved round the corner to 13 Britannia Street presumably for extra room for their growing family. Work was just a five minute walk to Davis Boatyard which was by the river. In 1928 Jimmy found work at the Cleveland Flour Mill.

Dad lived in Britannia Street when the 1921 Census was taken in a family of nine. Earlier his Mam and Dad lived in Carpenter's square where he went home from school one day and walked into the house and found another family living there, "Who are you ?" The folks had moved round the corner to 13 Britannia Street but forgot to tell him. At the time he was the only one in the family working. Dad was serving his time at Davis's Boatyard but on an apprentice wage so he had to leave to get more money doing foundry work. This would be in the 1920's during a downturn in the shipyards where his father and brother both worked, it must have been a desperate time.

Jimmy with workmates at the Cleveland Flour Mill pictured about 1950. *Dad worked as a packer but he did all sorts of jobs he was there from 1928 until 1960 when it closed, apart from his war service.*

Jimmy was at Belsen Concentration camp on liberation day 11th April 1945 when British and Canadian Troops found 13,000 unburied bodies and 60,000 inmates most ill with typhus and starvation.

He only talked about it once or twice over the years and it took me ages to get anything out of him. Dad was in the medical corps they'd heard rumours about this camp and after a small team did a preliminary visit, they were sent in to liberate the camp. There was a terrible smell and Dad couldn't believe what he was seeing, people were just speechless. The British soldier could usually make a joke out of any dire situation but everyone was stunned.

Left: A British soldier surveys one of the huge pits filled with victim's bodies.

There is some film of bodies being loaded, they put them on carts then in big heaps and they just bulldozed the bodies in to the pits. My dad is in some of the films that were shot. As Belsen goes it was a small camp compared to Auschwitz, Dachau and the like. As a Royal Medical Corps man Dad was not directly involved in the fighting but medics were allowed to carry arms to defend themselves.

Left: An inmate delousing. Many of the prisoners were Jewish, they included Anne Frank and her sister Margot who had both died in Belsen just a month before liberation.

The SS had managed to destroy all the camp files so erasing any documentary proof of the many atrocities before the camp was handed over to the British.

Huge problems faced the team in feeding the malnourished inmates who were too weak to digest food. Specialist teams arrived to devise the best way to feed the survivors.

I asked Dad about other incidents: occasionally the brigade would get an order instructing them not to take any prisoners for a few days and Germans would be shot out of hand. And once there was a sniper opening up on officers and killing lads from trees. They put a watch out for him but he made a mistake by starting at dawn – the flash of his gun was seen. He threw down the gun and put his hands up "Kamerad" There was a soldier next to Dad with a Sten gun, he cut the sniper in two.

One of the many Belsen graves, a photograph Jimmy brought home with him.

Studio portrait, Antwerp. Servicemen had photographs taken to send home to re-assure loved ones.

By pure chance Ken recognised his dad in this 1945 official photograph taken by a Norton based photographer many years after it was released. It pictures a bath parade in Antwerp: once a week the platoon went to the public baths from their site on the other side of town but one day the Liberty truck didn't turn up so they had to march there and back – hence the towels under their arms.

Left: Platoon marching through Antwerp 1945

Jimmy and Mary Payne (Pinder) with friends at the Village Club in about 1965.

Considering what he'd seen and been through he was a very well-balanced person and he was a good father and a good friend. I've often thought about post-traumatic stress and the effects. He rarely talked about the bad times.

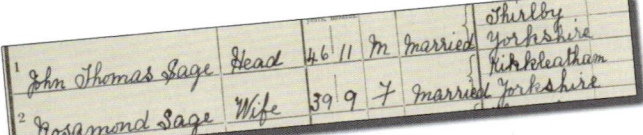

1	John Thomas Sage	Head	46	11	m	married	Yorkshire Thirlby
2	Rosamond Sage	Wife	39	9	7	married	Yorkshire Kirkleatham

CENSUS, ENGLAND, 1921.

SCHEDULE.

"That's nana holding auntie Winnie" explained Eileen Dobson **"She's standing outside 14 Short Street, we lived next door at number 12"** We found these photos in the Remembering Thornaby Collection now archived at Thornaby Town Hall and this provided some excellent background for our search because Eileen had deposited her family snapshots some years ago.

Centre: Rosamund Sage with her daughter Winnie about 1908 outside 14 short Street and on the same doorstep fifty years later.

John Thomas Sage married Rosamond Bosomworth in 1907 and they began their life together at 14 Short Street, Thornaby soon after. Rosamund Sage who lived to be 90 had been born at Kirkleatham Hall where her father John Bosomworth was a gamekeeper. John Sage came from the small Yorkshire Village of Yorkshire Thirlby and he was 66 when the Census was taken and recorded as an Electric Tram Driver.

"Grandad loved horses." Eileen told us. "He may have come to Thornaby from Thirlby to look after the horses that pulled the trams before the electric trams were introduced in 1898." However 1921 the year of the census is also the year the Electric Tramways Company closed so John would soon be out of work. It emerged that John was re-employed as a bus cleaner by Stockton Corporation Transport for several years until his retirement.

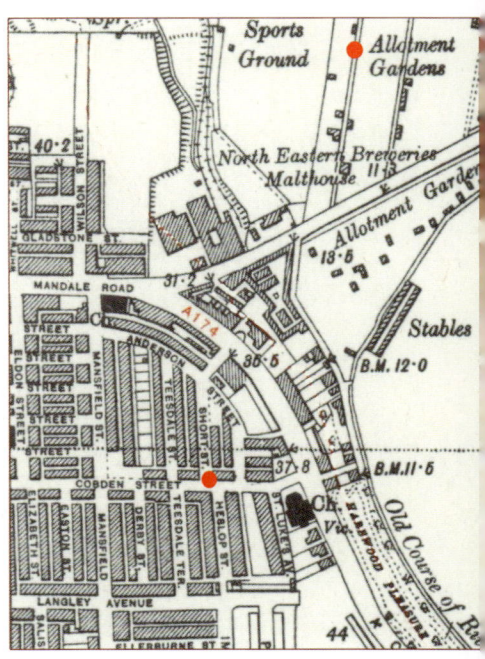

Grandad used to help out and look after the horses at Ringtons Tea depot which were just over the road to let the stable lad Ted have time off. He was brought up with horses and the land as a child that was all he knew so you can see why he loved his allotment so much.

Grandad never used to talk about work, all he was bothered about was his allotment and that was it.

Along Brewery Bank on either side of the Middlesbrough Road were two expanses of fine allotments and this is where John like so many others spent most of his retired life.

He was always at the allotment . It was smashing, folk kept pigs and hens and all sorts. Grandad had a beautiful spaniel and she loved peas. When the peas were ready she used to chew them and spit out the pods. Grandad played war with me one day and I said it's the dog and then we saw her. Then one day we got an eviction notice, both allotments were to be raised to make way for the British Rail depot although only one side was built on in the end so the allotments on the Racecourse side were needlessly destroyed.

A chap who lived in short Street used to invite us to his allotment to watch the races, people could watch from the Pleasure Gardens then they started closing the Pleasure Garden gates. Strikes also built an extension and it blocked the view.

Previous page, far left: Ancient and modern. We believe this could be John Sage driving his electric tram in about 1907. Before him is a Catholic procession headed by Monsignor Gerald Augustus Shanahan who led the Catholic community in Thornaby from 1877 to 1919.

Previous page, left: The allotments at the bottom of Brewery Bank were just a few minutes walk from 14 and 12 Short Street.

Right: Eileen Dobson with her grandad outside 14 Short Street in about 1950.

The allotment is what kept him going, you couldn't wish to meet a nicer person, nana was strict but lovely.

Parlour at 21 Stanley Grove, 1975. At the time of the 1921 Census this was the home of Arthur Fountain, a wood cutting machinist, his wife Mary Ellen, son Arthur and daughter Doris.

Snapshots of History

The War in Thornaby 1939-1945

Our book **Thornaby Lives** includes some fine photographs from Ann Peterson 's albums, now she invites us to look further into the fascinating collection of photographs she has lovingly preserved over the years: they are filled with social history. Old snapshots are always an insight into how we once lived, some might even be considered art. Ann's father Rob certainly had an artist's eye, her uncle Alf was also a keen photographer, together they have left a valuable legacy.

Above: Ann Peterson with one of the albums.

Right: Robert McWilliam Thomson, left, with his uncle's horses about 1930. Rural life offered few opportunities for adventurous young people like Rob and he is a good example of the movement to urban Britain during the 1930's. Rob soon found himself in Thornaby which he made his home for the rest of his life.

Dad took the photographs on the next few pages. Robert McWilliam Thomson was from a crofting family in Aberdeenshire but he had no idea he was heading for Thornaby, a town he'd never heard of when he signed up for the RAF. Anyway he was posted to Thornaby Aerodrome in 1936, met mam later on and the rest is history. Dad had a hard life on the Scottish farm, his father died when Robert was young and his mother brought up six children singlehanded together with a baby someone had left on the doorstep. Although three miles from a tiny school Dad managed to get a good education in the Scottish system and he used to help me out with my complex algebra when I was at school. They farmed seven acres of land and were self-sufficient, most importantly the Thomsons were a happy family.
Dad was incredibly hardy maybe the farm background toughened him, we never had a car in civvy life, he thought we were best walking, Dad biked everywhere.

Right: Robert Thomson in RAF uniform, a studio portrait by Forest Wompra, Middlesbrough c1940.

Above: Rob is posted to Thornaby where he remains, his snap of Thornaby airmen, summer 1936 with emergency vehicles. Behind them, a temporary hanger and left a distinctive " C Type " hanger is under construction.

Below: A Gloucester Gauntlet training plane c 1936.

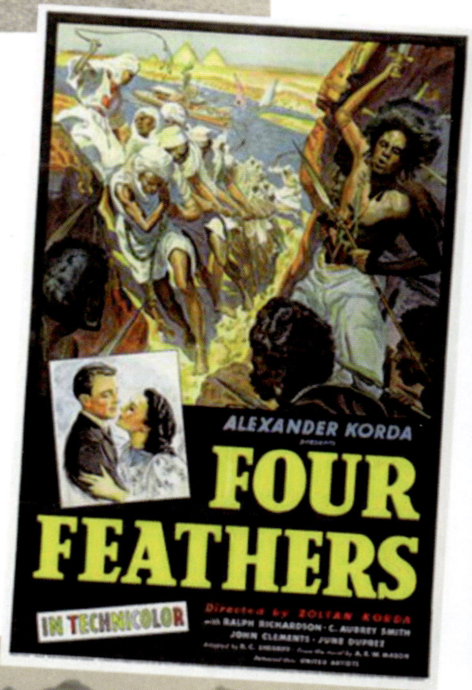

A witness to film history: Rob snapped some rare behind the scenes location shooting of the 1939 film "The Four Feathers." The epic war film set in the Sudan was known for its celebration of empire and spectacular battle scenes. The Technicolor feature was considered a great feat since the extreme temperatures were a challenge to both crews and actors.

Top: in pith helmet with back to camera is director Zoltan Korda talking we believe to Norman Pierce who plays sergeant Brown, about to be killed off in the film. On the platform technicians try to keep the enormous Technicolour camera cool, it used three strips of film at the same time: several miles of 35mm motion picture film were used.

Below: Rob's remarkable view of British actors getting ready for the advancing Dervish, played by local tribesman.

ALEXANDER KORDA presents

FOUR FEATHERS

IN TECHNICOLOR

Directed by ZOLTAN KORDA
with RALPH RICHARDSON · C. AUBREY SMITH
JOHN CLEMENTS · JUNE DUPREZ

Eyewitness: Rob's unusual candid snap of Amy Johnson refuelling at Wingfield aerodrome after her record- breaking flight from London to Cape Town in May 1936, it took three days, Amy only managed six hours sleep during several refuelling stops.

Right: a press photo of Amy Johnson, the famous1930's aviator who met a tragic end.

Rob's war posting to Africa This sequence of Egyptian scenes demonstrates how Rob was clearly a sensitive documentary photographer interested in recording ordinary people.

Dad was posted all over Africa during the war, Egypt, South Africa, the Sudan. He adored the sunshine and soaked it up. He was enthralled with the Pyramids and he befriended an Egyptian family who lived near the airfield. His photographs show how well he got on with people, we don't have a great deal of detail recorded about his war time adventures but the photographs tell the story. Dad had a busy war which included some harrowing moments when he was ordered to pick up body parts. Dad was brought back from Egypt in 1943 on the Queen Mary, the palatial liner which had been converted into a troop ship. I thought it was an incredibly lucky ship when you consider the threats from German submarines to this huge luxury liner where thousands of servicemen were billeted while they were transported home.

.

Another keen photographer in the family was Alf Bayles, Ann's uncle who was a builder with Coultas and Shaw the Thornaby Contractors.

Alf also helped to set up the Thornaby branch of the Red Cross at Peel Street with Wilf Thompson and drove ambulances for them. He was dedicated and a good citizen. He was a very shy man but when he gave lectures for the Red Cross he was quite interesting.
Alf loved taking photographs and did his hown developing and printing at home at 115 Thornaby Road where he lived with my grandparents until he got married at the age of 40.

Above: Alf Bayles snapped by a work mate repairing the roof of a maisonette at Gilpin Road. In the distance Elm and Beechwood Road.

Left: Alf on his motorbike with nephew Robert Thomson in the back lane between 115 Thornaby Road and Walker Street both demolished during the late 1970's.

Below: Sunday night TV at 115 Thornaby Road when Alf records a piece of social history illustrating some of the changes in late 1950's Thornaby. Television sets became more common in the town and 1959 saw the launch of a local ITV station, Tyne Tees whose popularity dramatically increased audiences.

TV was a revolution of sorts. Programmes like What's my Line the Brain's Trust, but ITV really opened it up with shows like Sunday night at the London Palladium, Good old Brucie he saved our souls.
Alf was one of the first to get a Television, set and after church nan would come home with her friends to watch TV. It killed the art of conversation though, you weren't allowed to talk. This is my grandparents on the right Clare and Fred Bayles with Mrs Bell from Sun Street and Mrs Johnson.

Alf was also a Civil Defence Volunteer and took his camera to many of the regular exercises and demonstrations, these are in East Cleveland during the late 1950's

Nuclear fears: a now almost forgotten volunteer organisation set up in 1949 to deal with the aftermath of a nuclear attack, nearly half a million people were active as Civil Defence Corps at its peak in the mid 1950's. They were disbanded in 1968.

In spite of doubts about the practical effectiveness of Civil Defence, Thornaby had many committed volunteers who enjoyed their roles and the camaraderie. Many national volunteers used their Civil Defence training in peacetime emergencies and disasters such as Aberfan.

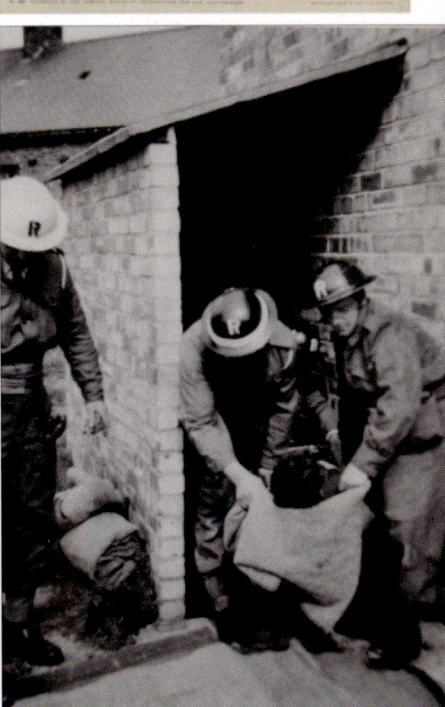

Our Corner Shops

In the old industrial end of Thornaby most of the resident's needs were on the doorstep with a corner shop on nearly every street. In 1939 Helen Crone set up what was to be a thriving business on the corner of Queen Street and Barnard Street. In a 2012 interview Helen's daughter Dorothy Toulson who died recently describes the work involved.

I thought it was the Black Hole of Calcutta compared to where we'd been at Norton. She said she was going to open this shop, and make it into a bakery, that was how it all started just before the start of the war. Mam was very strong, she'd battle for anybody who came and said they'd been bad done by she'd take her pinny off and be in like a lion. When people had been desperate and told her the tale she'd sort it out. My dad was a master plumber by trade but he liked his cigarettes, 40 gold flake a day. We saw him coming up the street one day holding on to the window sills. She got the best doctors for him, he must have lasted about 3 months before he passed on of Thrombosis.
Mam was one of six kids from Tilery, her mam had also been widowed early so she opened a shop to survive, Nana had a tick book even though she couldn't read or write, she lived to be 95 though. So the shop tradition just carried on really.

A lot of the rooms upstairs in the Barnard Street houses were let to people because no one could afford a house of their own then, it was a long time before people could buy anything for themselves. I remember VE Day in 1945, it was such a relief and joy at knowing you'd never hear a siren again and the anxiety it caused everybody. That's what caused mam's stomach problems, it was the anxiety of it all, because she was up at six o Clock every morning hail or snow to start baking. She'd open at eight o clock as a rule for breakfasts: teacakes and doughnuts, it was a tiny oven she used. The shop was a 24 hour job really.

Mam's shop on the corner of Barnard Street and Queen Street taken by Norman my husband in about 1969. One window had everything you can imagine in it, we even had chicken's one time, little fluffy things. The Queen Street window was always full of sweets. The milk bottles are waiting to be collected, Mam's mini is parked outside, and I think that's me in the shop. In the background on Westbury Street is Paleschi's house, they ran the ice cream business, next door lived the wet fish man Mr Fell and then next to him on the corner of Chelmsford Street was Mr Hall's coal yard, he was a cousin of my mother. The Austin Cambridge car far right belonged to Mr Page, Pages were popular general dealers on the corner of Westbury Street and Queen Street, his father had started at about the turn of the 20th Century. There was a sweet shop opposite Pages on the corner of Queen Street.

Mam would rest in the afternoon and have a couple of hours when it was quiet and one of us would take over. I don't know where everybody slept, I can never figure it out because there was only two bedrooms. You walked through into the back which was extended and had a covered bath, if the shop was closed: "Right we'll have a bath." As soon as you got water in the bath someone would knock and then you'd be running around with a towel trying to avoid them seeing you, talk about a pantomime.

People would knock at the backdoor: "Mrs Crone do you have a …." On the corner over the road was the fish shop run by the Davis's, he had been a Bevin boy. Mrs Davis was a lovely woman but full of arthritis, she picked the wrong job working with cold potatoes, just barrels of wet. She just deteriorated naturally with all her aches and pains. Me and my two sisters used to go over there for a bath on Friday nights because they had a big bath. They left the fish shop because she couldn't cope any more.

Mam sold everything including cigarettes, the apprentices from Head Wrightson always came for cigarettes and you'd sell them five packets of Woodbines. Then you'd have all your tins of biscuits on the

floor to be packaged along with rice and sugar tins. You had a cold place where you chopped the butter up and the lard. Then we got a fridge in and that was a tremendous step up because you could keep things longer. Mam was sympathetic to the customers who were having a lean time and of course there was a lot of tick, the main job was getting them to pay it back.
DOROTHY TOULSON

I had relations in Barnard Street so I was quite happy to move there it was the first house we ever had, bought for £500. It was nice and homely, everybody was friendly, Barnard Street was a smashing place to live. The thing I remember most of all was Mrs Crone's doughnuts. Whenever you talk about Barnard Street Mrs Crone's doughnuts come up. Everybody used to go to Crone's. I don't ever remember seeing Mr Crone, she brought those children up on her own, she worked hard for them.
WINNIE MCHUGH

We had a shop on the corner of Gilmour Street and Georgina Street which is where I was born along with my two brothers. The only role I had to play was occasionally stocking shelves and as an unpaid paper lad, every morning but I'd be able to go through the comics and read them as well . I started at the tender age of six or seven. They call them the good old days and they were the good old days but as much as I loved it I wouldn't like to go back because there was a lot of poverty. In my gran's shop there were people who couldn't afford food so they'd get it on tick until they could pay for it.

Previous shopkeepers at 77 Gilmour Street photographed in about 1930. Costello's bought the shop in 1941.

My mother Madge was Helen Crone's daughter and bought the shop around 1941 when my Father was called up for war service. She was the driving force in the shop and when my Father was demobbed he got a job while my mother ran the business, she loved the shop but it's beyond me how she managed to raise we three boys at the same time. Mam and Dad met in the Co-op Bakery before the war and the figure of £200-£300 comes to mind when the shop purchase is mentioned. We left Gilmour Street around 1957 for larger premises in Norton and then mam's sister Helen Porter who had established a shop on the corner of Charles Street and Hartington Street took over. Their shop which was also an off license was only half a block away from us. As a paper lad I was out into the pitch black every morning but I went to Westbury Street School which was just a hop skip and a jump across the road so there was no excuse for being late.
FRED COSTELLO Helen Crone's grandson

Below: the last days of George Street 1977. Jack Scott's paper shop foreground established by his father in 1897 Jack worked from 6am till 6pm most days until he retired in 1964.
Far corner, Howson's butchers was sold to an assistant during the 1960's by the Toulson family who established the shop in the 1930's. On the opposite corner of Barnard Street, Hogan's Flower Shop.

Centre: often a beacon of hope on the dark Thornaby nights, compact shops like this on the corner of Gilmour Street and Hartington Street opposite Costello's also sold medicinal supplies like toothache tincture and aspirins. With only a single room for provisions, corner shops were created using two large rigid steel or cast iron beams supported by columns at the entrance, these beams held up the rooms above. It seemed precarious but there were very few examples of collapsed structures. **Above left**: the popular family bakery on Peel Street and Charles Street which closed in the late 1970's. **Right** on the corner of Duke Street and Trafalgar Street next to the Commercial Hotel, a popular newsagent with Head Wrightson workers who dropped in for cigarettes and papers.

Below left: Matt Livingstone and Mrs Livingstone's tobacco and sweet shop on George Street proudly decorated for the 1937 coronation. **Right:** 1903, frame makers and glaziers at the George Street end of Georgiana Street. Some businesses were short lived, the lure of regular wages in local industry like Head Wrightson often persuaded small traders to give up. Jacob Smith's shop became a general dealer.

When the Trams Came to Thornaby

Whitwells Ironworks

Bone Mill

Site of Bridge Hotel

July 16th 1898: the photograph of an electric car crossing Victoria Bridge commissioned for the Tramways' lavish publicity brochure also captures long gone features of the Thornaby industrial landscape. The Bridge Hotel a local landmark is not to be built for another five years.

The North Eastern Gazette of July 14 1898 called it a "Great Tees-side revolution." It was the closing years of the Victorian age and the promising new town of Thornaby was just six years old, so how fitting that a truly modern transport system should be launched on Teesside. It reflected the confidence of new boroughs like Thornaby that were emerging and where the Electric Tramways arrived well before the London system was built.

The Trams made a huge improvement to the way we lived: here was a cheap reliable transport system that connected the main Teesside towns; as many as fifty electric cars served the route which meant that trams could turn up on a regular average of five minutes. The specially designed motor cars were capable of seating 60 passengers inside and out, they weighed six tons, were well lit with electric light inside and out, each car cost £800 each, an astonishing amount of money in 1898. A journey across the whole route cost a reasonable 3d while worker's specials were laid on each morning and evening at 1d a person. It now became possible to work outside your town and get cheaply and quickly to work.

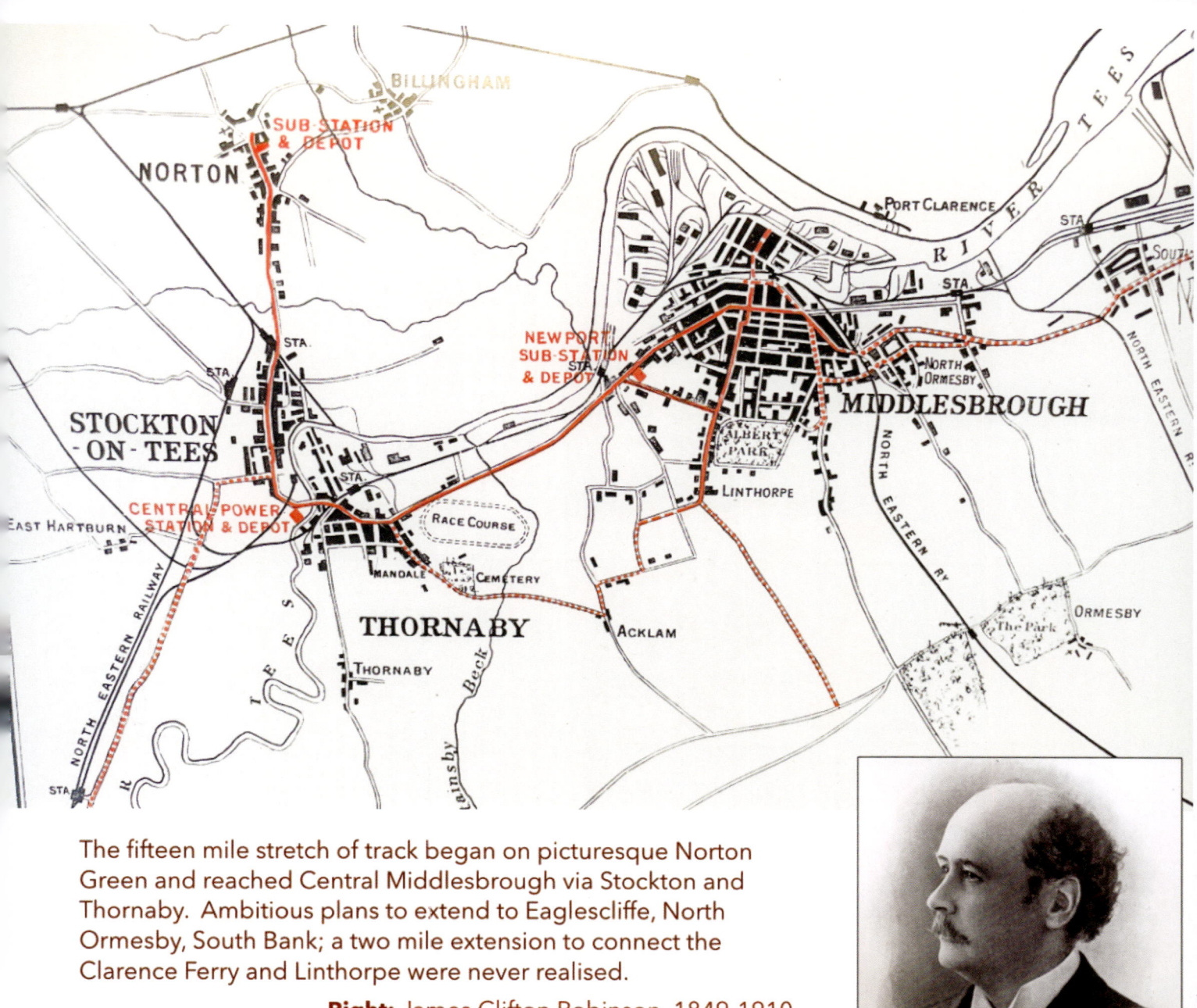

The fifteen mile stretch of track began on picturesque Norton Green and reached Central Middlesbrough via Stockton and Thornaby. Ambitious plans to extend to Eaglescliffe, North Ormesby, South Bank; a two mile extension to connect the Clarence Ferry and Linthorpe were never realised.

Right: James Clifton Robinson, 1849-1910

The trams enabled citizens of the neighbouring towns to mix more easily than before, marriages between people of different towns was now more common. Job opportunities extended courtesy of cheap and regular tram fares.

But who was the force behind this phenomenon? How did it proceed so confidently? In fact several systems including Bristol Tramways had already been constructed by the Imperial Tramways Company and they were the models for the Teesside success. The man behind it all was flamboyant Clifton Robinson, known as the Tramway King, involved in building the New York, London, Liverpool, Dublin, Cork, Bristol, Edinburgh and Los Angeles systems.

The Evening Telegraph of 16th July commented on the mutual strength the tram would bring the area: "The whole district is bound to experience a buoyancy as the result of this splendid development of communications. But the three towns especially are now knit together into greater homogeneity than has hitherto been possible and Middlesbrough and its neighbours more than ever form a great metropolis of the North East of England." The Western Daily Press added: " Within a month they had carried 700,000 passengers without injuring a single person. They had proved to the satisfaction of the community that they were to be relied upon. They had gained the confidence of the people. " There is no doubt the Trams far exceeded expectations but the installation timeline was astonishing.

Above: Construction gang, on the Wilderness between Thornaby and Middlesbrough. Perhaps the stern expressions shown in this photograph reveal the effects of the darker side of Clifton Robinson and his company: Robinson was said to have " Shown an arrogant disregard of economic realities when spending shareholders' cash and he exhibited an authoritarian insensitivity to the just demands of his workforce." One can only imagine the poor working conditions and meagre pay of these men toiling in the open in all weathers around the clock to complete the system on schedule.

" The first pick was put into the ground on the 1st September 1897. In spite of storm and stress the work went steadily on throughout the winter and was brought to a completion on 1st March 1898. The whole of the 15 miles of track was laid and there was no better tramway in the world; and the power house was planned and brought into operation within eight months. "
No wonder that when the three Corporations of Middlesbrough, Thornaby and Stockton were approached with the tramway proposal in 1897 there was some scepticism and the mayors of the three towns admitted later that they did not expect the promise of the promoters to be fulfilled.

The Central Power Station close to Victoria Bridge in Stockton had a river frontage and wharf with an electric crane so coal and other stores could be landed. The three condensing engines of 400 h.p. each made by Allis of Milwaukie were shipped from the USA. Water was drawn from the river Tees to operate the condensers and the boiler feed pumps. The three dynamos generated 300 Kilowatt each.

Mandale Road scene, inauguration day July 16th 1898. Crowds gather to watch in the streets and they crowded into the cars to get their first day ride. **Right:** 1898 promotional brochure.

Two weeks after inauguration Clifton Robinson and the directors surveyed the whole of the tram system by a special car decorated with flowers . "In the power station, lunch was partaken and the party afterwards adjourned to the terrace by the riverside. "

In 1921 the local authorities took up an original option to buy the system and Stockton and Thornaby councils ran the trams themselves, much of the infrastructure needed updating. Meanwhile, competition from the developing motorbus companies had been a constant throughout the twenties and one can see why, buses were more comfortable compared to the relatively spartan trams and routes were more flexible. This alongside the personal motor car revolution filled our towns with vehicles.

Contrary to initial fears that our citizens would be electrocuted, few were harmed by trams while safety features like sensory fenders prevented people from falling under the wheels. The characteristics of the trams are legendary: the noise of screeching steel wheels in the tracks, the rattle of the cars and the regular flashes of blue light from the conducting wires, all created a romantic attraction to trams. So in 1931 when the last tram ran thousands turned out to say goodbye. The trams had served Thornaby well for over thirty years. Now over the last quarter of a century trams have been rediscovered as an efficient and environmentally sound mode of transport: trams run on electricity and do not pollute. Years of pollution and congestion by cars and motor buses have taken their toll, imagine what some of our teeming cities would be like today had the trams survived.

Unidentified group outside the Royal George Hotel on Thornaby Road and Sun Street, C1912 and left, the scene today.

This fine photo of regulars at the Royal George Hotel on Thornaby Road was brought to our stall at the Thornaby Show by Jerrod Henry. Not many of the 30 or more pubs that thrived in the town survive today but they were the glue that held the community together and cornerstones of community life. Pubs were often managed by strong characters who were well respected, this way of life was not for the faint hearted though, tenants were tied to the building 24 hours a day, it involved heavy physical work and businesses often only thrived if an extended family were on hand to help out with endless duties and tasks. Jack Green's grandmother Celina Hall told him that she and her mother had morning jobs at the George preparing it's several coal fires and black leading the surrounds, for the George like many others opened early to serve passing industrial workers before their shifts began. This all changed at the start of the First World War to a relatively draconian schedule of Luncheon 12pm - 14.40pm and Supper 18.30pm - 22.30. The government feared Alcohol consumption would affect war production so access was dramatically restricted and remained in force until the 1980's.

We know that publican Frank Bower died intestate at the age of 56, in 1921, but the trophy and the reason for the gathering remain a mystery. The George is now student accommodation, we are sure it's rooms could tell many stories.

A group of regulars with landlord and landlady in the front room, 1974

The Bon Lea appears to have been the Brewery tap for the nearby North Eastern Brewery which was on Brewery Bank. The pub was popular with customers working at the Bon Lea foundry at the end of Reed Street and Hoppers rope works. The young man in this early 1930's photo attending his families' ice cream cart is Carmine Paleschi.

Thornaby's Lost Pubs

At the top of Brewery Bank, The Harewood Arms, named after the main Thornaby landowner, was popular on Race days and later for the British Rail depot which was further down the Middlesbrough Road. The Harewood had a Buffet Lounge which women were allowed into but not in the bar. Post war this pub was run by Thomas Turner and grandson Stuart Bell sent this reminiscence: *Vaux Breweries made him landlord after serving at the Station Hotel opposite the Town Hall during the war. Thomas was taken prisoner by the Germans in the first war and he became a victim of a gas attack in which he lost a lung and damaged the other, so due to ill health his wife Ann became licensee. I remember watching Granddad tapping beer barrels in the cellar, he was known in the area for his good pint. Upstairs was a kitchen and living room with an open fire where they lived most of the time but it was enormous with a long landing, with rooms all along, at the end was a huge parlour where the family gathered and where we always spent Christmas. Thomas died at the Harewood Arms in 1959 aged 69.*

Thomas Turner, publican

Above, the spacious Commercial Hotel opposite Thornaby Station, below left The Bradford Vaults, Trafalgar Street.

The area called "Below the railway" was the industrial hub of Thornaby, and it once supported seven pubs: The Ship Inn, The Bradford Vaults, The Collingwood, The Burton, The Rokeby, The Commercial and The Cleveland. Workers from the foundries and Head Wrightson and earlier the two shipyards numbered nearly 2000 and many needed to restore liquids lost in the hot and heavy industry. The Commercial and the Collingwood were finally swept away by the Teesside Development Corporation in spite of protests but the Cleveland Inn is now the popular Dubliners. Below, Collingwood Hotel regulars join the Walker sisters Georgiana and Eva, fourth and sixth from left in the final days of their tenancy. The sisters ran The Burton Hotel also on Trafalgar Street opposite until 1957 when it was demolished to make way for a Head Wrightson car park. Eva Walker (Maiden) who ran a popular juvenile dance studio and troupe died soon after this photograph was taken in 1976.

Thornaby based North Eastern Breweries sold off all of it's pubs many to Vaux during the late 20's depression and produced an inventory of photographs of the properties, some like the Golden Fleece were copied and they have become valuable records. The misty view reveals the effects of Thornaby's many coal hearths and industrial chimneys. Like it's neighbour The Duke of York or the Black Bobbies as it was affectionately known, the A66 swept up the Fleece and all properties along the East side of George Street in the late 70's. Far left is the entrance to the National School. David Allport photographed Cameron's Brewery draymen delivering to the Windmill in about 1978 when the Inn was about to be compulsory purchased, another casualty of the A66 dual carriageway. The contemporary Street View shows the vegetation that has sprouted up on the site of the Windmill Inn, this mound supports appropriately, a prolific apple tree.

THORNABY-ON-TEES, VICTORIA BRIDGE, SHOWING TOWN HALL.

The Last Days of the Bridge Hotel

Nancy Skelton contacted us with photographs from her late father Eric Brigham. Eric and Dot his partner were licensees of the Bridge Hotel, living in four rooms there during the 1950's and 60's and we recorded her remarkable description of one of the town's most popular landmarks. Proudly standing, at the entrance to the town the Bridge Hotel was the first building you encountered after crossing the bridge. The scale and quality of the construction of this elegant residential hotel suggest the Bridge was created for more prosperous times which may never have actually arrived. By the time the Brighams took over in the early 1950's the top floor set aside for guests together with a huge function room were derelict. Nancy tells us

" I always remember when you first walked in they had a huge roaring fire burning, everybody used to sit around the fire. It was the same upstairs in the bathroom with a lit fire in it. All the coal had to be moved about, there were big coal fires and we had to bring the coal up and down the stairs in scuttles, it was a huge place. I was terrified of the cellars, you would probably find a rat if you went down there, it was near the river and there was a separated staircase that led right down to the river. I can imagine what it was like when the Bridge Hotel was first built, it was beautiful. The draymen were the only visitors to use the top rooms on overnights before the long journey back to the Beverley Brother's Brewery in Wakefield."

The Dunkirk spirit: a group wait to be evacuated from the beach at the end of May 1940 not knowing whether they would survive or not, yet some raise a smile for the camera. From a set of six images given to Nancy Skelton by her father Eric Brigham showing the devastation.

Eric was a natural publican, he regularly played the Bridge piano and earlier ran the Alma in Dovecot Street and the Buck in Guisborough this is where he was given an hour's notice to accommodate 200 soldiers who had survived the retreat from Dunkirk. One had snapped scenes of the evacuation with his box camera but probably too exhausted to do anything with them. Eric had the roll of film developed and Nancy Skelton inherited six postcard prints printed from the negatives. Eric was soon to become a soldier himself but returned to doing what he loved best after the war and ran the Alma Hotel in Stockton before the Bridge. Sadly Eric died on a visit to Sheffield to see Nancy and Dot Brigham ran the Bridge on her own for two years, it was a lively warm place says Nancy and during the early 1960's Dot set up popular Blues nights on Friday's with John McCoy. On her own she was terrified at times though by this foreboding but once elegant building and it's ghosts.

A difficult load from Head Wrightson emerges from Bridge Street onto Bridge Road in front of the hotel in 1957

Left: The Bridge Hotel bar in the late 1960's. Right to left, barmaid Una, Dot Brigham, licensee, Daughter Nancy Skelton who had a career as a successful vocalist and toured with the Kaye sisters. Dot took on the Bridge Hotel after Eric Brigham died.

Our thanks to Marilyn Proctor.

Parades Gone By,
Thornaby Ceremonies.

A range of fascinating annual events have drawn the people of Thornaby out onto the streets over the years and for many they were the highpoint of the callendar to be looked forward to whether as a participant or spectator. One was Mayor's Day seen here, however the last of these popular processions took place in 1967 just before Thornaby Borough Council was wound up and the town became part of the short lived Teesside Borough Council.

Thornaby Borough Council Macebearer G.R. Groves leads the Mayor's Day procession along Westbury Street in 1957. A day of great pride, this was a chance for residents to see the new Mayor but there was also an element of accountability: the ratepayers were able to see who was responsible for spending their money and providing their services. Here Mayor Tom Padgett is accompanied by long serving Town Clerk Albert Stockwell together with members of local services and clergy. On the far right the Bell family at number 24 turn out to witness the march past their home.

Overleaf, photos and memories of the spectacular Corpus Christi ceremony which ended during the 1990's. The Catholic May Queen procession still flourishes though and many residents say they are often moved to see young people of eleven years old tour St Patrick's church singing Marian hymns like "Bring Flowers of the Rarest" and to witness the Queen crown the decorated statue of Our Lady with a garland. The May Queen herself, Lilly bearers, basket bearers as well as bearers of the May Queen's long train are all proud members of the procession.

Mayor's Day about 1956.
The procession began at
Thornaby Town Hall and has now
reached Thornaby Road bank. In the
far distance the Cleveland Flour Mill.

The above photographs were taken from outside 115 Thornaby Road by uncle Alf Bayles my mother's brother who lived with us. I well remember Alf taking them because I was standing beside him, I was eight years old and this must have been in about 1956. The Royal George would be just out of shot to the left and there's Sun street where the corner shop is. This was the Mayor's day, it was a massive, real occasion, in those days you had all the forces taking part and we had our own Mayor. The procession is going to St Paul's church for the service. I think we respected events like this, it was something to be proud of, everyone turned out and it all felt very ceremonial with his worship and all the councillors leading the procession, I think there was some colourful people then. It also shows what we had in Thornaby, people were proud, Thornaby was a very proud town, it still is.
Anne Peterson

I was born in 1937 and made my first procession at the age of five. I remember the excitement, it was like a festival day, although it was a catholic ceremony and had meaning for us, it was very much for the whole community, people of all faiths and people of no faiths, they all came out. Then after the procession on the school grounds at St Patricks Primary School there was a benediction, it was a social event.

In Westbury Street they'd have bunting all the way up across the street and some of the residents who lived at the top of Westbury street with the bow windows used to put statues and flowers in them and make a little altar at the top. I remember looking up and seeing these beautiful statues in the windows. It was very much a highlight for us as kids to walk but in the schools were quite strict about us all being dressed properly. Most of my family were catholic, my other grandma and aunt weren't but to them it was still a big day, not just to see me and my brother walking. You know I can't remember it ever raining, I can only remember the sun shining. The procession was dedicated to honouring the Blessed Sacrament, Corpus Christi means the body of Christ. Four people carried a canopy and underneath would be the priest holding the monstrance, which contained the blessed sacrament. We regard this as the body and blood of Christ, it's carried to spread the blessing. I was part of every procession until the main one stopped during the 1990's. First we had a lot of bad weather, then they built more onto the Primary School where we gathered, so for a number of reasons it stopped. Also some felt traditions were gradually changing all over Britain which was gradually being considered more of a multi faith community.

Kath Crossan

This was my first Corpus Christi at the age of five, in the above photo I'm on the left with Josie Dunn and behind me my friends Jacqueline Dawson who was my best friend and Angela Jones. I always used to cry because there was so much preparation involved: those little white shoes were hard to find then and the veil and gloves alL had to be immaculate. My first dress was made by my Auntie Elvira Costello from her own wedding dress which was beautiful, it came from Italy. Dad used to put the veil and gloves in a plastic zipper bag ready for the following year, I wasn't allowed to touch it.

Angela Costello

I wore white socks and sandals, the dress was off me mam, me mam's friend had three daughters and I always got her cast offs, that was second hand dress, the headscarf was my sisters, my mam always kept it, it would have been about ten years old. I got brand new shoes and socks and the beads belonged to my dad, dad always had rosary beads so he give me his rosary beads to carry.

Left: Corpus Christi, 1969, school friends Angela Costello and Josie Godwiin

Right: Angela Costello and Josie Godwin in 2023

I remember lining up in St Patrick's church and we all got paired up, I got paired up with Angela, I knew her from school class. But then about a year later we were rehoused and moved onto the new estate I went to Christ the King school. But then when we were put back together at St Patrick's secondary School, so we became really good friends. And then I met John who was her cousin and ended up marrying him. You just felt great on that day because you weren't used to getting dressed up. I was about six years old there. I think that's Angela Riley on the right. All our kids followed the tradition they were all in the procession. I remember us all being gathered together and being so excited and putting the veil on was really special. Then we were living in Cuthbert Street just a few streets away, with tin baths and back streets, it was only a two bedroom house but we used the parlour as a bedroom, I always remember the tin bath and outside toilet. Years later my husband John was in the procession, he wore white Jesus sandals and marched with a banner which he said was heavy, he had converted to Catholicism. We often wonder where all the banners went, they were such a part of life and so many people used to come out and watch. A lot of work went into it but it was that older generation that did it and they've mostly died off now.

Josie Godwin (Dunn)

I was born in 1963, my mother had six miscarriages, in those days the doctor used to give her internals, today it's ultrasound examinations. So when she knew she was having me she didn't go to the doctors, because she used to blame these internals for the miscarriages. My god mother Katie Divine who lived in Glasgow Street was going to Lourdes, so my mam wrote this petition out to our Lady "I'd love to conceive a baby." She knew she was pregnant but didn't go to the hospital, she didn't go anywhere. When the time came mam went into Park End Hospital for me to be born and the local doctor said " I don't know how this lady can have produced a baby in her condition." Mam had a duodenal ulcer and was only six and a half stone, I was a miracle baby, and that's why they believed in Lourdes.

My dad visited St Patrick's every day, he was devout. His coffin rested inside overnight before his funeral. Cannon Breen, got out of his sick bed to say my dad's requiem mass the next day. Dad had had lung cancer so he used to sleep in my bedroom with being poorly and I slept with my mam in their room, he was too weak to come downstairs. He had had his lung removed at Lord Byron's in Seaham Hall hospital in about 1973. He was alright for a few years then he got a shock because next door had a fire, there was all the noise and commotion and I think that set off the cancer again. About eleven o clock one night we were getting ready for bed, "Good night God bless" And we went in his room and he was gone. He's not here ! My mam said "Come on I know where he is" And we found him kneeling on the steps of St Patricks church in the rain, he was praying.

Norman Costello and Margaret Costello (Fulton) visit a Catholic shrine in 1960

Top: a procession on Mandale Road passes Eldon Street.

Below: past Queen street on Thornaby Road. This busy junction disappeared in 1978 and is now part of the A66 dual carriageway.

Royal Visits

Right: Mandale Road 1977, one of two Royal visits to Thornaby. A previously unpublished photograph of spectators waiting for the Royal limousine to pass by.

Many Irish Catholic people came to industrial Thornaby for the promise of a better life during the 19th Century and they brought their traditions such as Corpus Christi with them. Left, images from three Corpus Christi processions at the turn of the twentieth century. Seated left in the open landau in these pictures is the Rt. Rev. Monsignor Gerald Augustine Shanahan who served as Parish Priest at St. Patrick's Church during the important years of Thornaby's early development from 1877 until his death in 1919. Gerald Shanahan came from Kilfinanne in County Limmerick, his three brothers also became priests.

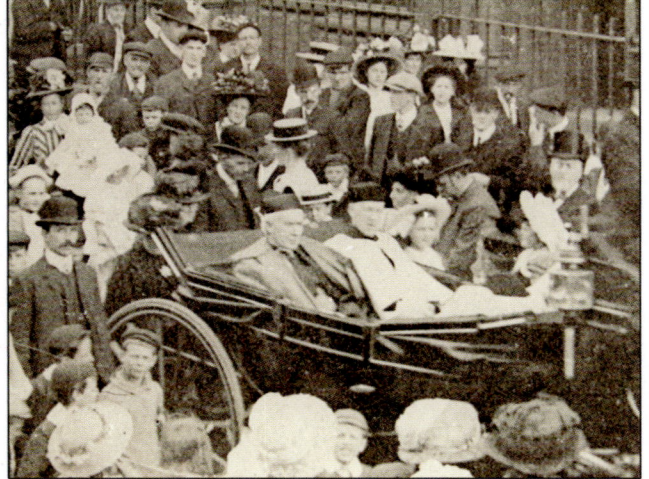

Right page top:
1977 Royal Visit on Mandale Road cleared for the Queen's limousine and her journey to Teesside Park Racecourse. Special constables get ready to take their positions along the route to control the crowds, although compared to the 1956 visit this is considerably smaller, much of the population having moved to the Airfield estate. The north side of Mandale Road on left is about to be demolished.

Bottom: British Legion members headed by Mary Walker at possibly the 1957 Mayor's Day parade. The ex-servicemen's medals suggest many experienced an intense active service during the second world war.

Left: Mayor's Day parade on Mandale Road 1961

This is me, centre carrying the flag in the 3rd Thornaby Guide Company. We used to meet at the Thorntree Road Baptist Church and each year when a new Mayor was appointed we were part of the parade. In 1961 I was chosen to carry the Guide flag and it was a moment of great pride. I had started in the Guide movement as a Brownie at the 3rd Thornaby Brownie company in 1951, then progressed to The Guides after the age of 11. I've continued in the movement until today as a leader and now in the Great Yarmouth Trefoil Guild for retired guiders. I remember Mrs Hendry was the Brown Owl and Guide Captain, she was dedicated to the movement and also a member of the Baptist Church. There was no shortage of youth organisations to join these parades, there was the Boy Scouts, Boy's Brigade and all the cadets, there was always something for young people to get involved in. My boyfriend Colin took the picture, a few years later we were married.

Lilian Watts (Reeve)

PHILIPS
J·ROUND & SONS Ltd
KETTLE
CHARLES INGLE
KEN JACKSON CAR SALES

Tweets from the past

Postcards were similar to modern tweets on Twitter: short messages to keep in touch. For a small sum you could send a message to a relative or friend and guarantee it would reach them in the UK the next day or remarkably even the same day, since Royal Mail once had two collections and two deliveries a day ! Most importantly you could also send a nice picture to illustrate the message. Millions of cards were posted every month and fortunately for posterity millions have survived along with their messages, they are often rich in historical detail.

Stockton-on-Tees - Durham

The most interesting things here are the Shipyard. The boats may be seen in every stage of construction from the bare frame to the finished Article, but that applies to most towns here

STOCKTON-ON-TEES.

The River Tees at Thornaby c1890. This printed card taken from Victoria Bridge has a further layer of social history because of the message about the shipyards, written when yards were booming. Craig Taylor's yard is in the distance on the right, in the foreground the Carrs field once a racecourse, is now the Victoria Shipyard.

V314-4   STOCKTON-ON-TEES. FERRY BOATS, RIVER TEES.   RAPID PHOTO E C

This Postcard from about 1905 is a "real photograph" and represents what our writer was describing: shipyards and heavy industry are thriving on both sides of the river, at Teesdale and Portrack and beyond. The image captures the worker's daily routine of heading to and from Thistle Green on the Stockton side to Trafalgar Street over in Thornaby. The celebrated Kelly family ran one of the ferries until the 1960's.

Right: Taken from a room at the busy Windmill Inn on the corner of George Street and Mandale Road, a hand coloured card captures a scene in about 1910.

Middle: Few Thornaby people had telephones so postcards were often the only way to get messages out cheaply and quickly. We'll probably never know who J.B was but their message warns friends of a visit to Bedale on 16th December 1905. Census research should reveal more about the milling Hobson family at Crakehall.

Below: A pen pal sends a picture of Mandale Road to her friend in the town of Mende, in the South of France region of Lozère. Erminie would have found the card a contrast to her own small rural townscape, the trams especially were an innovation in 1903 when this card was posted. Georgina of 27 Westbury Street was also trying out her French, her history can be discovered relatively easily using sites like Ancestry.

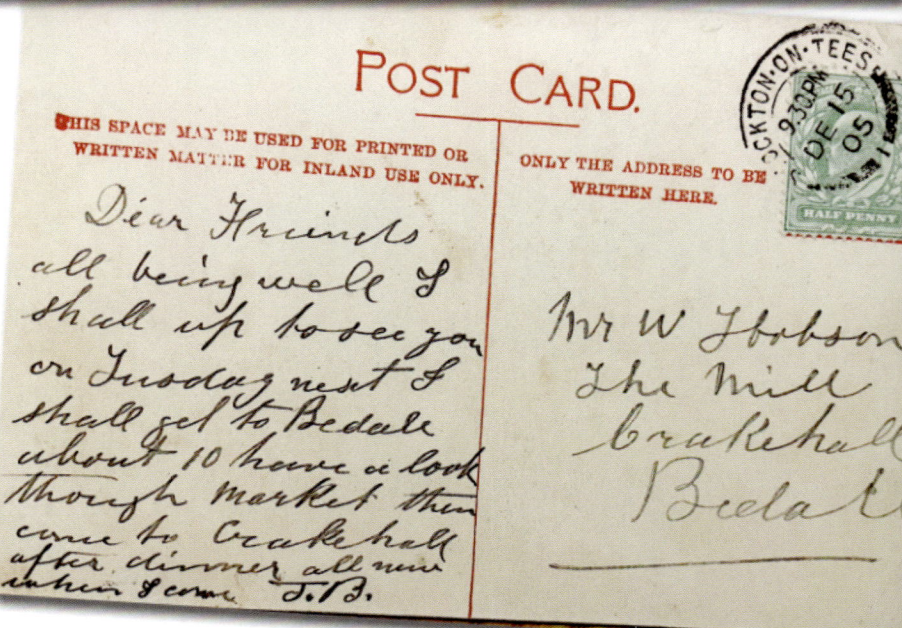

R.C. Clifford the Linthorpe photographer has gone to great lengths to turn his 1910 photograph into a work of art, even having the oval image embossed. However, the scan below from the original half plate glass negative reveals some important figures have been cropped out in the process, but it also shows an enhancing sky has been skilfully inserted. Clifford was a talented photographer who obviously engaged well with local people: many figures in the crowd have been arranged, it remains a masterpiece among images of Thornaby and probably unique in having a surviving negative.

Five Lamps.   Thornaby on Tees.

Taken from exactly the same position outside Paleschi's Ice Cream shop, the photographer from Valentine's may be trying to copy Clifford's earlier postcard. The Valentine postcard issue number tells us it was taken in 1911. The horrors of the World War awaits some of the younger men in 1914.

JV 67418   **FIVE LAMPS, THORNABY**

This favoured vantage point of a popular scene inspired many postcards over the years. Taken about 1906 this was posted in July 1909 by the mother of Mr. W. Wilson living in Richmond, her simple message assures him that all is well in Thornaby.

Taken in 1933 by Valentines the intervening years have seen the demolition of both the Pure Oil and Cake works and the Bone Mill and construction of the new Cleveland Flour Mill. Apart from this relatively little has changed.

Postcard publishers asked their photographers to seek out timeless scenes and avoid cars assuring the card a longer shelf life.

Disaster cards like this of a collision between two trains at Thornaby in 1907 were an early form of news and they were often issued in large runs to meet demand.

RAILWAY SMASH - THORNABY. M.I. 5/07

Robert Thirlwell of nearby Bridge Road, one of our best local photographers, might also have been commissioned by either the railway or insurance companies to record the scene for legal reasons, issuing the card later.

J. BRAITHWAITE, Builder and Contractor, Gilling House, Thornaby Rd., Thornaby-on-Tees.

Trade cards were an effective form of publicity, they have also left us with records of a vanished world. Produced in about 1910 there are few visual records of building in Thornaby even though thousands of homes were created. John Braithwaite 1858-1939 lived at 19 Gilling House on Thornaby Road and appears to have been helped in the business by his son John, a joiner.

ALL STEEL WELDED BEDPLATES
FABRICATED BY
HEAD. WRIGHTSON & CO. LIMITED.
THORNABY-ON-TEES

A quality card from the 1930's produced by the marketing department of the world class Head Wrightson Engineering at the Teesdale works. The card provides an unusual view of the busy Bridge Yards and also reveals how primitive conditions were without proper cover: workers toiled in the open in all weathers.

Demonstrating the incredible range of products that originated at the Trafalgar Street Head Wrightson works this is one of many steel fabrication contracts the firm won during the 1930's.
The Edgbaston cinema opened in 1937 during a period of major art-deco picture palace construction in Britain. The Bristol, later an ABC, enjoyed a long and distinguished life, closing in 1987.
The site is now a MacDonalds drive in restaurant.

BRISTOL CINEMA, BIRMINGHAM

Steelwork fabricated and erected by
HEAD, WRIGHTSON & CO., LTD.,
THORNABY-ON-TEES
CINEMA STEELWORK A SPECIALITY

Community events involving large groups were viable postcards for photographers because the participants usually bought copies: The 1937 Coronation Barnard Street party taken by C.W. Kipling of Stockton at St Luke's Hall. Families represented include: Appleby, Fulton, Haycock, Peak, Buxton, Scott and Tunney. Many individuals in the group have been identified.

Cards like this early 1930's Five Lamps scene by Thirlwell's of Stockton are now avidly collected. The card is printed on doubleweight silver bromide paper, it could have been a short run because originals are now scarce: one turned up on Ebay recently and fetched £110.

Below right: The photographer from Francis Frith Ltd captured the heart of a town whose people were just recovering from austerity and six years of war in our 1953 card, probably the most widely seen image of Thornaby and probably the best loved.

Today prints can still be ordered from the company which has preserved much of the 150 year output from this legendary firm documenting the face of Britain where often a postcard is all that remains of a once thriving scene.

Thornaby-on-Tees, Five Lamps & George Street.

Caught in Time

Taken nearly 70 years ago by the Francis Frith Company this postcard remains one of the most familiar and probably the most popular of all Thornaby images. The scene has long gone but we have identified five of the people recorded in the photograph along with some background to tell the story of the 1953 Frith Postcard.

The Five Lamps, this is where people of Thornaby met, the Salvation Army Band played and New Year revellers danced. For many residents it was considered the heart and soul of the town.

Rita 1928-2017 and Jim Bartley 1919-2014 in Whitby two weeks after their marriage in 1948.

Rita Bartley 1926-2017

"In the summer of 1953, Mam told us she had seen the guy with his stand and big camera outside the butchers on Mandale Road, he was obviously a professional but she didn't see the results until a postcard appeared in the shops in 1957. It is just possible Mam was returning from The Welfare on Francis Street after hearing she was pregnant with myself. Mam left her job at Pumphrey's to have me in 1954." Tony Bartley.

"Mam had been working at Pumphrey's" Explains her daughter Sandra. "She'd been walking past and saw

Above: Rita in her garden at Clarendon Road 2010

Winny Porter one of her friends who was going for a job there and she joined her. Jim had helped to build a new part of the mill as an apprentice joiner when old John Pumphrey saw him work and offered him a job. Dad served as an almond miller until war service when he was one of the last people to be evacuated from Dunkirk. He returned to Pumphrey's with PTSD after being demobbed and began dating mam. She used to change the silks for the icing sugar and worked on a special consignment of icing sugar for the Bowes Lyon cake for the Queen's wedding. Mam finished her working life in the Delicatessen at Woolco in the 1970's" "We've just discovered 300 wartime letters between mam and dad which we hope to do something with, they are full of fascinating historical detail like descriptions of the bombing in Thornaby.

Tony Bartley reveals more about his father's escape from the hell of Dunkirk in the following chapter.

s, Five Lamps & George Street

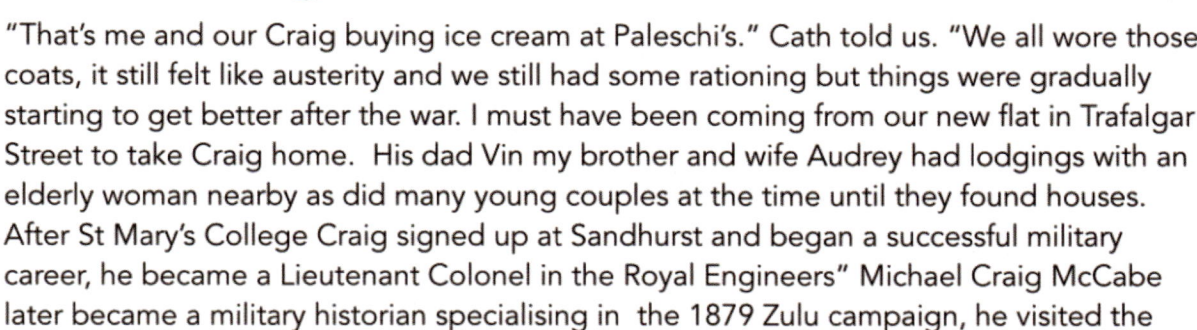

Cath Harrison and Michael Craig McCabe

"That's me and our Craig buying ice cream at Paleschi's." Cath told us. "We all wore those coats, it still felt like austerity and we still had some rationing but things were gradually starting to get better after the war. I must have been coming from our new flat in Trafalgar Street to take Craig home. His dad Vin my brother and wife Audrey had lodgings with an elderly woman nearby as did many young couples at the time until they found houses. After St Mary's College Craig signed up at Sandhurst and began a successful military career, he became a Lieutenant Colonel in the Royal Engineers" Michael Craig McCabe later became a military historian specialising in the 1879 Zulu campaign, he visited the

sites of the conflict and researched the families of Zulu warriors involved. Cath b.1933 made a great contribution to the Remembering Thornaby Group who inspired a campaign to preserve the Thornaby identity, they not only gathered valuable archive photos of the town but listed the Town Hall and prevented Thornaby Station from being named South Stockton. Michael died in 2013 aged 63 in Andover.

Left: Craig aged about eight. **Right:** Cath working at Head Wrightson 1951. **Below:** Cath on the Teesside Princess 2012.

Howard Fulton 1901-1974

A moulder who was invalided out of the Bon Lea Foundry in 1947 with pneumonia and never worked again, Howard lived round the corner at 11 Barnard Street. At 52 he would have been younger than the mainly retired men he sat with some of whom would have been first world war veterans. The Lamps was a popular pastime for many retired men like Howard and strong friendships often formed there. Henry Fulton, Howard's father set up a bakery business where Hird's is on the right of our photo in the early 1890's when he arrived from County Tyrone in Ireland. However regular wages in local industries were more attractive especially in bringing up a young family.

Howard returned to the lamps in 1973 but he found it impossible to reach the steps because of the high speed traffic now routed down George Street.

Toulson's

Along with Williamson's and Proctor's this was one of three butchers in a row at the top of George Street. Meat including cut price offal was a staple diet until the 1970's when more diverse foods became available. Nearly every part of an animal was butchered, sold and eaten including intestines and stomach linings called tripe. Right: Emeline and Ed Toulson with staff outside the shop decorated for the 1937 Coronation.

Dominic Paleschi
1880-1973

In homburg hat Dominic can be seen by his premises on George Street. Liborata and Domenico arrived in England from Sora in Italy at the turn of the century. "Grandad had a good reputation for quality and for being clean and hygienic which meant a lot when you were making ice cream, even the yard was scrubbed. All the sons and daughters contributed to the business and as a consequence it flourished." Remembered Albert Paleschi. There was some Home Office confusion over his naturalisation papers and Dominic was interned on the Isle of Man at the outbreak of war for 18 months as an enemy alien even though his children served in the war effort some with rank. Soon after the photograph was taken the Paleschi's introduced a juke box at the coffee parlour which soon became a mecca for young people. Many Thornaby couples did their courting in the shop during the 1950's.

Blooms

Isadore Bloom born 1864 in Russia set up the well known Pawnbrokers at 84 George Street. Isadore gained naturalisation in 1894 so we believe the shop was established just after. One of four similar shops, the business survived after his death in 1925. Bloom was grand master of the Middlesbrough Masonic Lodge and a prominent member of the community.

Right: Tommy Thompson the last manager with pledge book photographed in 1973. Marked by two decades of severe unemployment caused by the failure of major industries in the town during the 1920's and 30's people resorted to pawning their valuables. Blooms also sold clothing and domestic goods.

The Wilson Family

The Wilson's overlooked the Five Lamps area from this room which was part of their extensive home at number 1A Barnard Street in the street to the left until the late 1960's. The 1939 group portrait was taken in Devizes just before the move to Thornaby. In 1941 Jim Wilson seen far right, was knocked down and killed by a United bus almost at the spot where our Frith photograph was taken from. Jacob and Elizabeth Wilson were also offered the empty corner shop on George Street when they took on the tenancy of 1A but decided to run their second hand clothes business from a Stockton Market stall. The unit became Hogan's the florists. The whole block was demolished in 1974 to make way for the A66 dual carriageway.

The Constitutional Club

The popular club also known as Smokey Joe's moved to this shop unit at 72 George Street in 1938. Ian Murray the present Treasurer has researched original minutes going back to it's inception in 1934 and they make interesting reading. Ian discovered for example that Harold Macmillan later to be Prime Minister stood as a guarantor for a £200 loan when the club moved to George Street with debts of £168 and this was possibly used to pay them off. The club was popular and active in fundraising for various causes over the years but didn't become debt free until 1970. In 1979 the Constitutional moved to their newly built club house in Cheltenham Street.

The club substantial entrance. On the next corner is the Conservative Club or "The Cons" this building could take more members.

The club in 1974

Scott's

Jack Scott 1897-1991 began work for his father at the newsagents seen far right in the postcard, he was only seven when he began delivering papers, eventually he took over the shop. Jack senior originally wanted to lease one of the units along the side of the block until a friend told him a corner shop was always a prime site, the advice paid off and Scott's became one of the busiest shops in Thornaby, Jack retired in 1964 but the business survived until the 1970's.

Who were Frith's ?

Our photograph was one of thousands of precious originals just a week away from being bulldozed when the Francis Frith Company went into liquidation in 1973.
Francis Frith photographers toured Britain taking scenes for postcards, the collection is now regarded as a priceless record of the country . Original prints going back to the 1870's and many precious negatives were saved from destruction by photography editor Bill Jay who recognised the collection as a priceless national treasure. Now catalogued and lovingly restored, The Francis Frith Collection remains active after over 160 years. Prints can be ordered from the Collection through their website.

Copyright The Francis Frith Collection

The Frith photographer took this other view down Mandale Road on the same visit.

Jim Bartley: Escape from Dunkirk

Many Thornaby service people were affected by the horrors of their war experiences. Jim Bartley was one, based on interviews recorded just before he died, Jim's son Tony writes of his father's role in the Dunkirk evacuation when the British Army in France was nearly lost to the invading Germans. On 29th May 1940 Jim was rescued, one of 338,000 soldiers to be saved from the disaster.

Once the Germans decided to break out in May 1940 Jim was gradually pressed back to the coast. This is where it became very hairy. On one occasion, he crawled his way, in his truck, through roads teeming with Belgian refugees and took refuge in a Red Cross Hospital in the grounds of a brewery outside Ypres. He parked and scrounged a cup of tea. An Officer came up and asked him what he had in his lorry. "200 tank mines," said Jim. "Right, bugger off and get the Hell out of here," said the Officer, so Jim did. He got half a mile away and in his mirror he saw the chimneys of the brewery collapse in a huge sheet of flame. The Field Hospital had taken a direct hit and was no more. As the situation became gradually more desperate Jim was assigned to taking shells and ammunition to the troops manning the last line of defence around Dunkirk, which was nicknamed "the ring of steel". It was a very thin ring indeed and Jim felt acutely uncomfortable driving away from these men, knowing full well that the next vehicle these troops would see would be German. He got lost one day and stopped in a clearing to grab a bite to eat. After a few minutes a French Policeman on a bike rode over waving his arms madly. The Germans were in the next village half a mile up the road! Jim turned round. Soon the order came to make for the sea and it was very much every man for himself. On one occasion Jim was in a convoy of canvas sided trucks when 9 ME109s, straffed the convoy, three planes targeting the vehicles and three either side straffing the men as they ran into the fields either side. Jim remembers seeing the bullets hitting the ground just in front and behind him before a huge explosion shook the ground. One of the ammunition lorries went up and Jim saw the cab describe a graceful arc through the air straight towards a church steeple, which was promptly chopped in half. When he got back to his lorry he had to put out the flames of the canvas sides, or his load would have gone up too.

He was told to make for La Panne, where he was to ditch his lorry into the water to make temporary piers (so the troops could get onto the fleets of little boats rescuing the men off the beaches.)

Top right: troops wait to be picked up from the beach.

Left: soldiers use tanks for shelter as they wait to be evacuated. All of the army's equipment was abandoned or destroyed, 90,000 men were never picked up.

Right: lifeboats used as pontoons to reach the rescue ships.

Far Right: Jim was one of over 2100 men rescued by HMS Harvester in four trips over three days while under fire.

Some distance out of La Panne German Bombers attacked his convoy. He noticed an airfield on his right and a monastery on his left. He went for the monastery and cleared a 7 foot hawthorn fence. One explosion took him off his feet and flung him about 20 feet further on, but as his legs were still running, he landed mid stride and carried on. Some of the drivers in the convoy made for an outhouse, Jim and Glen made for a door in the monastery. He took shelter under the door lintel and saw that the room he had entered was a refectory with a long table set for a meal. Suddenly there was a huge explosion and a wall of flame and heat rushed past Jim's shoulder and scorched his uniform and the whole building shook. Jim thought it was coming down. It didn't. When the smoke cleared the table was bare and outside there was a huge smoking crater where the other drivers had taken refuge. Jim arrived on the beach at La Panne amid chaos. He drove his truck into the water and decided to walk to Dunkirk. He said it was horrible. Men who had looted rings and watches were dead crushed under vehicles that had sunk in the sand. There was very little cover and the beach was constantly under fire. He said he was more afraid of the unruly troops than he was of the Germans. When he arrived at Dunkirk he stopped on the steps of a picture house and, using the can opener on his jack knife, he opened a tin of bully beef he had found scattered on the road. It smelt awful, so he threw it away. He looked inside the picture house and realised what the smell was. It was a temporary mortuary. The whole floor was piled 20 bodies deep with the corpses of soldiers. He got outside and literally bumped into Lord Gort (the Commander of the evacuation) who told him to stand at ease. Gort advised him to make for the East Mole of Dunkirk harbour, so he did. The mole was under constant fire and gaps in it were covered with planks. Jim missed two destroyers, which was just as well, as both were sunk in the Channel and at about 5 pm he ran along the mole in a group of 20 and was unceremoniously bundled (by two sailors) through the air and on to the deck of HMS Harvester 12 feet below! The deck was at a constant angle as its guns were firing, Once there, more sailors slid him out of the way and he took refuge in the galley, Someone gave him a condensed milk tin full of tea and he watched the cook roasting beef whilst shells passed up the hoist just behind him to the turret above. The Harvester made only two trips to Dunkirk saving 1341 men that day. Jim was on the last trip.

When he got back, he celebrated his 21st birthday, his hair had gone white.

It took him a long time to put Dunkirk behind him; PTSD was not known then. Jim carried little back from Dunkirk: he had his rifle, backpack, his knife, webbing and what he stood up in.

Denis Alexander Smith working at the kitchen table on "Mandale Road Folk 1979." The painting is now owned by Lord Wrigglesworth.

The People's Painter

Denis Alexander Smith

Many Thornaby people will have inexpensive prints by this prolific artist who believed in distributing his work widely, Denis created over 300 works altogether during his relatively short life as a painter, they were sold at modest prices to visitors at his regular exhibitions.

Denis Alexander Smith left school at 14 in 1943 with ambitions to go to art college but like many of his generation he had to go out to work and bring money into the home and Denis started as a shipping clerk. So began a lifetime of varied jobs and occupations that was to take the artist across an unusual range of occupations. During a five year spell in the 1960's for example he was variously engaged as a deck hand on a river Tees dredger, he became one of the region's first bingo callers, at the Stockton Empire then at the converted Queen's Cinema. Denis was also salesman collector for a credit company on some of Teesside's most notorious housing estates.

Nearly 40 years on after being made redundant from Teesside Textiles in the early 1980's and then in his final retirement, Denis was able to achieve his goal to paint every day, and he eventually became a respected local painter whose exhibitions of Thornaby and Stockton's industrial past were hugely popular over the years. It didn't happen overnight though and apart from a few terms at Teesside College of Art Denis was self taught: he would paint every brick in a scene rather than suggest them which a trained artist would have the skills to achieve; he struggled at times with colour and composition; he never really mastered the colour palette and his work often strayed into the sentimental but his work struck a chord with many people in Thornaby, they liked to have all those bricks for their money !

When Denis died in 2002 he left behind a collection of completed and unfinished works in his studio and this treasure trove preserved by his family, contained many of his favourite paintings of subjects that were dear to him. Denis held an affection for the people and places he painted and we can see this in scenes of Thornaby and Stockton that have now vanished, they represent the best examples of his work.

Denis is on the left in this snapshot which captures one of the artist's many jobs in local industry, here he's seen at Lionweld Kennedy on Stockton Riverside during the 1980's. Below "The Forge, Lambert, Smith and Storr." One of his finest paintings and also a self portrait as Denis features himself operating the forge hammer used to shape hand rails for a power station. This was he wrote " A momento of my time at Kennedy's, most marked by a rewarding sense of camaraderie."

In 1993 Denis retired from his final job as a courier driver for Cleveland County Council and spent the rest of his days painting. It is tempting to imagine what Denis might have achieved had his parents the means to send him to art school at thirteen when a talent for drawing was clearly emerging. Like many gifted young people of his background his creativity remained buried until uncovered by a virtual accident forty years later. His example shows how someone with very little in the way of resources but with talent could create memorable pictures.

The painting called "House on Charles Street" below is typical of Denis Alexander Smith's skill in populating scenes with his own figures and stories. Denis discovered the print of what we believe was the caretaker's house to Westbury Street School just before demolition. He was inspired to recreate it's past as a once proud building with tenants around 1959. On the right is the artist's family, wife Frances Fulton who was a pupil at Westbury School and is seen pushing daughter Linda in the pram, son Derek is on the right. Depicted on the left is Howard Fulton, a great uncle of Frances who the family lodged with in Barnard Street. There was an acute housing shortage in Thornaby at the time and many newly weds lodged in the front rooms or back bedrooms of relatives until they found suitable accommodation, there was to be a long wait for many families until the airfield development solved the crisis with the creation of 1000 new homes in 1965.

Seen again in close up Howard Fulton stands on the footbridge to Thornaby Station in about 1960. Howard was a moulder at the Bon Lea foundry just across the tracks to the right of the station and began there aged thirteen but he was invalided out with chronic pneumonia in 1946. Howard believes this was caused by him regularly emerging into the cold air after a hard shift drenched in sweat. Howard had lost his own family to tuberculosis during the early 1930's.

A tribute to fellow artist L.S. Lowry. We know Lowry visited and painted Teesside so Denis thought it appropriate that we should find him waiting for a train at a place he would certainly have liked and probably have seen, the magnificent Thornaby Station.

The approach to Thornaby Station at the turn of the twentieth Century, an area with a lot of memories for local people as Denis later wrote: "They went down it to their work, they went down it to the seaside, they went down it to war. " Based on a well known photograph taken from Thornaby Town Hall in 1903, Denis has again filled it with his own figures and detail such as the Cadbury's Cocoa enamel sign which was a feature of his back garden for many years until it rusted away. The only building to survive this scene is the Cleveland Hotel now The Dubliners, seen on the middle right with green facia.

Right, ferryboats on the River Tees at Stockton. This thoroughfare down stream from Victoria Bridge was busy especially at the end of the main day shifts on both sides of the river as people from Stockton went to work at the shipyards, foundries and Head Wrightson and those from Thornaby to Ropners and the many foundries on the north side. Denis painted several versions of this scene and he was delighted when one was bought at an exhibition by the family of Jimmy Kelly who ran the last ferry boat across the Tees. Three generations of Kelly's ran ferry boats and the passage was a lifeline for many at this time who paid four old pence a week for their transport. On the left ships are under construction at Ropners shipyard on the Stockton side. On the Thornaby river bank two major shipyards: Craig Taylor and Richardson Duck employed nearly two thousand men at their peak. The post 1918 years saw a slump in demand and by 1931 most of these slipways were derelict creating mass unemployment.

Right: this snap of Denis in his back bedroom studio in about 1998 reveals how he managed to work so much detail into his paintings, he is seen with a strong magnifying glass and a very thin sable hair brush. Denis rarely worked in oils preferring watercolours, a medium that enabled fine detail. Above: blow ups of the Station Approach painting show the results of this painstaking technique: they are individual paintings in their own right.

A thriving scene on Mandale Road at the turn of the 20th century in a relatively new town created by Royal Charter in 1892. The foundries, shipyards and factories teemed with jobs when there was full employment. Many of these figures are from Denis's own imagination except the couple foreground right who are in fact the artist's parents Laura and Jim. The snap was taken during their courting days in the 1920's so not contemporaneous with the main scene but Denis might be forgiven for this effective artistic license. Below: we spool on nearly a century to Denis's photo of a ceremony inside the Thornaby Town Hall

itself when "Reflections of a Bridge" a painting commissioned by Thornaby Town Council is presented. Far left Mayoress Jean Kitchen, middle is Dari Taylor MP.

When Denis died these two incomplete paintings were found on his easel, significantly he had returned to memories of his childhood in his late years and here based on a snapshot is the artist with his mother and grandmother at Redcar in 1930. Below, Stockton Races in the early part of the 20th Century, an unfinished painting of an activity Denis loved - horseracing. The painting's present state took months to reach and shows how much time and effort Denis invested in his works. The potential for this to become one of his best paintings is clearly there. Bottom right the drawn outline figures show great promise and this is also one of his largest works measuring 30x40 inches on the best watercolour paper available which suggests how important the work was to him. Sadly this was not to be fulfilled since Denis had a heart attack in the late 1990's and although he made a recovery after having a by-pass he was unable to return to painting. Then years of smoking untipped Players cigarettes finally took their toll and he was diagnosed with lung cancer in July 2002 and died on August 30th at home. It is hoped to exhibit the entire contents of Denis's studio at some point in the near future.

The Mayor of Alegia de Oria and his partner treat Kenny Trainer and Jack Green, right, 1955.

The Kindness of Strangers

In the summer of 1955 three plucky young Thornaby lads set off for the Continent hitch-hiking without a map and with about £17 each.
Jack Green tells us about his remarkable adventure in a Europe before mass tourism.

My mate Kenny Trainer's Merchant navy ship had finished it's journey in San Sebastian, Kenny had stopped to explore the area a bit and he told us how nice the local Basque village people he'd met were, so we all decided to go hitch hiking there to see what it was all about.
Kenny Trainer, Tadgy (Terrence) Hobson and me got the boat train across to France. Tadgy was a Catholic and wanted to see Lourdes so first we walked and hitchhiked to Lourdes. It was absolutely marvellous, the processions, the Grotto, the people with leg irons who'd been cured. I brought a bottle of holy water back and a St. Christopher medal. From Lourdes we headed to the Pyrenees and Spain. We camped on one of the highest parts and you could see snow on the peaks but we managed to find a tunnel through the mountains which saved a lot of effort but it was full of cattle sheltering from the sun, big flies were biting us as we walked

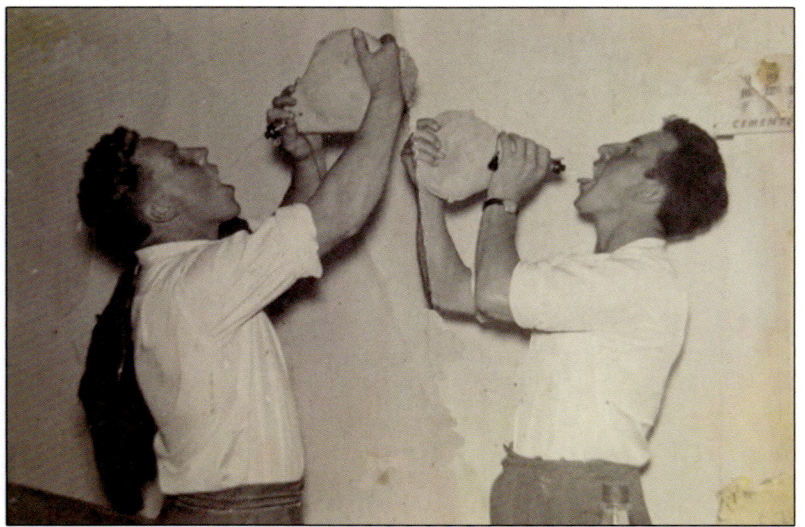

along. When we saw a lake and waterfall at the other side we took all our clothes off, no trunks on or anything ran down and jumped in. Next day we heard there were all these lasses from one of the villages looking through the bushes, so we had a good laugh. We rarely got lifts on the whole journey and we'd walked right through the Pyrenees to Spain which was quite an achievement.

The Basque village of Alegia de Oria. Today the Basque people with their own unique culture, language, have more autonomy but achieved years after the death of General Franco.

We stayed in a beautiful Basque village for a week, it was only a small village called Alegia de Oria but they were all really friendly people, the men all wore black berets. Outside the village they used to set up goat fights and they'd charge each other like expresses. They also had boxing in the village every morning and they'd let two bulls loose. We were only 19 then and I don't think the village had seen any English people before, the kids used to follow us all over. We were like stars for the week. Two days before we were due to leave the mayor of the village put us up in his restaurant where we drank and ate for free, the family really made us welcome. It was nice to sleep in a bed for a change. We used to go to the Fiesta dancing with the lasses from the village. The kindness of the people we met all over was so touching.
But before I set off Dad said " Watch out for Franco." You had to be careful because the Spanish Militia had a presence in every village with their Sten guns but we weren't too worried. The Fascist dictator oppressed the Basque people who had always wanted their own separate region, Franco had banned Euskara their language, no one was allowed to speak Basque.

In some of the villages it was just like being in a spaghetti western, ancient agriculture like two big oxen pulling the carts. It was just like the wild west, we ended up in Pamploma, where even to this day they let all the bulls run in the street. We camped just outside the village by a stream and we slept there for a couple of days in our sleeping bags. We stopped at San Sebastian our intended original destination for three days and went to two bullfights and swam in the sea there and eventually made our way to Bordeaux in France. We got on a train and did about 300 miles, would you believe on just a ten bob note.

General Franco, centre, meets Adolf Hitler in 1940, Hitler had supplied weapons during the Spanish revolution and notoriously bombed the Basque town of Guernica on Franco's orders. Franco continued to oppress the Basques under his Fascist regime which survived after the war until his death in 1978.

A parting photograph before setting out for San Sebastian: Jack Green and Kenny Trainer with the Mayor of Alegia de Oria's family and a friend in 1955.

We were walking around the square at Bordeaux when this chap approached us, maybe he was attracted to the big Union Jacks on our rucksacks. The gentleman told us he had fought against the Germans as a pilot. He seemed keen to tell us about the atrocities the Germans had carried out in France during the war. Again the kindness we had encountered in the Basque country prevailed and he invited us back to his house, they were lovely people, he put us up for the night there and treat us to a meal and wine, we had a nice bath and got a bed to sleep in and slept like a log. His beautiful daughter took us in to Bordeaux the next day to look around the town.

We were hoping to hitch a free passage on a merchant ship at Bordeaux port across the Channel but couldn't get on a boat so hitchhiked up to Calais to get on the boat train. We eventually got to Kent and we filled our pockets full of cherries from the fields, we slept in our bags amongst the poppy fields. A kind furniture van driver dropped us off at Lords Cricket Ground, then we got a lift from three British Road Services wagons each of us in separate wagons which took us to Yarm Lane corner. That £17 lasted me all that way, we lived like lords and I even had enough to bring dad a box of cigars back and my mother a musical decanter.

When the Thornaby lads arrived in Bordeaux the town had recently hosted a tribunal into the Nazi atrocity at the French village of Oradour-sur-Glane. We believe this is what the Bordeaux pilot who welcomed the lads talked about: On June 10th 1944 the Waffen SS herded 247 women and 205 children into this church, they sealed it then set it on fire. Several residents escaped through windows but were machine-gunned to death, as were the 190 men of the village.

Back to work: Jack, left, apprenticed at the Teasdale Brother's yard on Boathouse Lane, Stockton about 1955. The respected firm of agricultural engineers based in Darlington had been established for a century when Jack joined designing and manufacturing their own brands of machinery.

I had to start work again the following week and soon got back into the routine going to dances, there was that much to do for teenagers in them days. It was nice to get back, it was summer too. A lot of the farm machinery was still being pulled by horses during the 1950's, there was tractors but there was still a lot of horse work with ploughs, and grass harrows. The Combine harvesters were coming in just as I was coming out of my time, but there was binders and thrashers. It was a good trade, you did blacksmithing, welding, gas welding, profile burning, fitting, you had a good all round trade and I was learning from older tradesman who were extremely skilled. A lot of the farmers would visit on Stockton Market day to view and put their orders in. You had different seasons for different machines so you never got fed up. Then in December 1956 I was called up for National Service in six months I was on an adventure abroad again – serving in Cyprus but that's another story ....

Jack in Cyprus 1956

Spirit of the Stone
The Dibbles Bridge Memorial

It took over two years to complete, was 47 years in the making, but now finally the people of Thornaby have a fitting memorial to remember their loved ones by. This is the story of the Dibbles Bridge project from it's inception to the unveiling of the memorial on the anniversary of the crash on 27th May 2022.

Thornaby Town Council commissioned a documentary to raise awareness of this nationally forgotten event which remains our worst road accident and which is still keenly felt in the town. We estimated a ten minute short might fulfil the brief, perhaps featuring one of the survivors - if we could gain their permission. I imagined most of those involved with the crash would be difficult to trace. How surprised I was then to witness a huge story unfold as the various players involved came forward to be filmed. It began with Brian Dooks the celebrated Yorkshire Post reporter who was the first journalist on the scene, then an invitation from Lincoln Seligman whose garden the bus landed in, to film his memories, thoughts that had remained unspoken for over 45 years. The 49 minute film interviewed 29 people directly linked with the event and it became a valuable record of the disaster's background. Bi-monthly screenings on Together TV a popular national TV channel ensured that Dibbles Bridge would be remembered. On Youtube it reached a world audience with ninety thousand views and increasing.

Coldstones Quarry by Stephen Dinsdale © 2022 Stephen Dinsdale   https://www.stephendinsdale.com

However Thornaby Town councillors were concerned that no memorial existed either at the scene or at Thornaby and both sites were investigated. We visited the spectacular Coldstones Quarry, just over the road from the disaster site and the idea of a limestone monument took hold. Quarry manager Richard Green and myself were sent out to find a piece that might be suitable for our Thornaby memorial.

Out of hundreds of shards on the quarry floor we discovered a triangular slab about the height of a tall human figure, with a flat crystalised face, perfect for our purpose. A plaque could easily be fitted on the face whose surrounding crystals would sparkle in the light, it was certainly unique and an unusual find. After checking Richard revealed that his company would be happy to donate the limestone piece.

Top right: Richard Green searches for a suitable stone.

Right: an unusual wedge of limestone is found amongst a pile at the bottom of the quarry.

Below left: the selected stone is stored at the Quarry H.Q until needed. A Daler board template is used to determine the size and position of the plaque, held in by props because of the extreme winds.

Right: the spot chosen by Thornaby Town Councillors for a memorial overlooking the crash site. The kink in the road suggests the recurring cause of accidents. Sadly permission was refused by the landowner.

Right: Balfour Beatty lower the stone into the base. The over four ton piece was a real challenge to keep perfectly vertical so a lifting hook was bolted to the top.

Costs to the town were a fraction of the final bill because main engineers Balfour Beatty were able to include the memorial as the community element of a major project that had just been completed on the Mandale Road rail bridge nearby. Engineers from Stockton Borough Council worked alongside them, their combined efforts delivered a piece of extremely high quality.

Architect Michael Atkinson had done some impressive work on the Town Hall restoration so he was a natural choice to design the base. At the start of the year areas of pavement were cleared for the installation. It would demand all of the skills Balfour Beatty and Stockton Engineers could muster, the accuracy of the final segments for example was critical to within a fraction of a millimetre; the limestone weighed over four tons and precautions had to be taken to ensure that it would not sink over time.

Meanwhile work on the metal plaque continued to an initial design by myself.
William Lane Foundry in Middlesbrough would cast the final item and offered advice at each stage. A key challenge was creating a 3D pattern from my 2D drawing. Traditional moulding once involved highly skilled carpenters to make the accurate wood patterns, now Computer Numerical Controlled (CNC) machines do all the work where a drill is connected to a computer via links to a 3D version of my artwork, the drill cutting out either metal or plastic. Our final pattern was made in Perspex by Croft Casting at Whitby, who produced an accurate pattern with tapered letters.

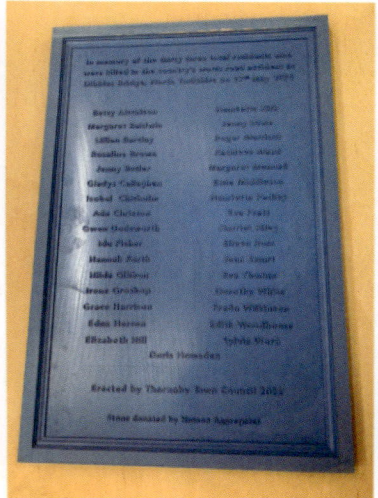

William Lanes Foundry led by CEO Stuart Duffy cast the plaque using the Perspex pattern to make a sand core for the molten metal. Potential threats from scrap metal bandits almost persuaded us to opt for the cheaper aluminium but bronze was chosen in the end being more suitable for memorials, and most importantly, more durable. Stuart and William Lanes contributed their labour to the project.

The bronze plaque is cleaned up with steel wool and soapy water after being released from the core. A vintage patina could have been created using hot wax which effectively ages the bronze but it was decided to leave the plaque to develop a natural patina of it's own over the years.

David Tinkler of Rose Memorials, Middlesbrough cuts a recess into the limestone block for the plaque to sit in. This is for aesthetic reasons but also to deter any scrap metal thieves from attempting to steal the plaque: the high initial adhesion of the polymer that Rose Memorials used behind the plaque will make it impossible to remove.

Jamie Thomson and David Tinkler of Rose Funerals and Memorials complete the plaque setting which is immediately covered up ready for the unveiling ceremony the next day. Jamie's company gave their time and materials free to the project.

Left: far left, an example of CNC machining. Middle image, this version of the text proved too thin to be cast. Next, William Lanes made a sample cast of one of the final patterns in aluminium, however the lower small bottom letters break up so a bolder font is used for the final casting which was in Bronze.

Guests came from far and wide to the ceremony on 27th May exactly 47 years after the disaster. The two sons of Jenny Butler one of the victims are examples of those who made great efforts to travel to the ceremony, one came from Worcester, both are in their tenth decades.

Left: new Mayor Ian Dalgarno removes the purple velvet cover sewn by Sylvia Walmsley from the stone.

Left: for many it is an emotional time as Reverend Robert Desics reads out the names of all the victims during the dedication ceremony.

.

Left below: The two grandchildren of Ena Hill, Cindy Davies and Diane Huitson who travelled from Kent. The reception was held in the Council Chamber and guests were able to view the completed restoration work on the magnificent Town Hall building.

Right: After nearly a century of accidents, a warning sign is finally erected this year at the top of Fancarl Hill which is where many travellers start their fateful and often tragic descent to Dibbles Bridge itself, responsible for 44 deaths since 1925. Three cyclists have been killed there since 2015.

Four key responders of the Dibbles Bridge tragedy: Lincoln Seligman, (in the above photograph) and the three campers from Hull, Stephen Jennison, Steven Griffin, and Carl Dickinson. All four were already at the scene when the bus landed and they stayed to help the injured until all passengers had been removed from the site to Airedale Hospital in Keighley. In the group photograph a relative talks to the three campers, many of the relatives were keen to pay their respects to the four responders who became unsung heroes of the tragedy.

New memorial lists names of 33 people from town who died at Dibbles bridge in UK's worst road disaster

Memories of day out in Dales that ended in tragedy

DIBBLE'S BRIDGE
Long, steep descent
Cyclists test brakes
& ride carefully

16%

Try your brakes

Right: The event is widely covered by the press. Both memorial and town hall represent a dream fulfilled by the Thornaby Independent Councillors who were responsible for the projects success.

Bottom Right: in the refurbished Town Hall Ian Dalgarno and Rev. Robert Desics stand by the new Thornaby Crest painted by Steve Badger.

70's scenes in Kodachrome

Colour slides of early Thornaby are rare, exposures had to be spot on for the shots to work, and it was expensive, so often the domain of enthusiastic amateurs. These examples are taken on Kodachrome, a costly film because processing costs were also included in the price but Kodachrome was celebrated for its rich colours and permanence - as these photos now testify forty years on.

Top: 1977 The People's Mission on New Street is about to be demolished.
Right top: Thorntree Road 1975. Today there are no fruit and veg shops left in Thornaby. Above: Peel Street looking towards Francis Street 1977, clearances for the A66 have begun at the bottom along Queen Street. Right: November 1970 Durham Street has just been demolished along with Wellington Street. Through the gap is Queen Street School. On the corner of Queen Street and Whalley Street: Miskelly's shop with Mr Miskelly's car.

Above: bonfire slide courtesy of Frank Mallon

Top left: Coking coal on it's way to British Steel passes the Middlesbrough Platform of Thornaby Station c. 1977.
Middle: The old coking plant c.1977, the "Torch" was used for washing coal.
Far right: Station Street c.1977
Left: Mandale Road 1973. The south side was later demolished and the road widened, the Town Hall now has a fine forecourt as a result. Cycling home after Sunday overtime at Head Wrightson is Stan Carlton.
Bottom left: A familiar shot of Thornaby Station c.1975.
Right: J.Rounds garage, Reed Street c1975. Bottom Right: Stanley Grove c.1976.

MILLER'S PLACE during the 1919 Armistice. This cramped cul-de-sac off Gilmour Street, didn't get much light into its small two bedroomed homes. Albert and Mary Jane Sexton lived here with their large family from 1910 until 1934 when Albert's Sweepstake fortune enabled the parents to move to Thornaby Green, son Robert took over the Miller's Place home at number five.

Miller's Luck

Golden Miller

A big win was to many people during the great depression the only way to find release from their situations of often poverty and overcrowded homes. Albert Sexton achieved it in 1934 thanks to the Irish Sweepstake when he won the equivalent of £750,000 today, at the time it was a fortune. Albert's granddaughter Audrey Henderson recounts this remarkable story of good luck:

You know when you pick a horse if you are not a real pundit you try and pick something in the horse that you are familiar with and the family lived in Miller's Place which is probably why he picked Golden Miller. It was the Grand National and the famous horse had done well at Cheltenham. Granddad signed up with the Northumberland Fusiliers, Yorkshire Regiment in 1915 and when the war ended he became a labourer then an engineer, he worked at Ashmores in Stockton which is where he bought the ticket. There was seven children in the small two up two down house at number five Millers Place, Albert and Mary Jane are recorded there in the 1911 census with five children my mother Hilda was one, born in 1903 The two of them moved from Miller Place to Thornaby Green after he won that money, a row of new semi-detached houses were being built and he bought one outright and called it Miller House. The inside of the house on the Green was very posh to us, and it had a beautiful garden. The toilet was upstairs which was posh to us. Mary Jane my grandmother had it beautiful, like my mother she was spotless. She used to wash the surplice for the choirboys from St Peter's church on the green.

Google Street View

MILLER HOUSE

Newly built in 1934 on Thornaby Green this was like moving to paradise for the Sexton's but it was soon to be re-mortgaged, in spite of Albert's substantial winnings. A family wedding c 1936. Mary Jane my grandmother second from right, Annie the youngest daughter, third right. Albert second from left and inset with son Stan next to groom we could be son Robert.

Below Albert and Mary Jane at Redcar in about 1950, most of Albert's fortune had gone by then.

We were poor because my mother had nine children and a husband who had bronchial asthma. The other couples were given ten pound each, my mother only got ten pounds and we were the ones that needed it most. Unless he shared it with lots of others we don't know about. He could really have bought that whole row on Thornaby Green and set his family up in something. With my father being an invalid we knew poverty. Granddad was known as good old Albert because he used to go to the aerodrome and gamble his money away and drink it, until there was nothing left. I don't think he was thought of as good old Albert then. The men there happily parted him from a lot of it: Gambling, card playing and beer drinking, we don't know where the rest of it went to but it didn't go to his family. He maybe had favourites. I think he had to re-mortgage Miller house so son Stan and his wife bought it off them probably in the early 1950's. Albert and Mary Jane who had cancer went to live with their youngest daughter Annie. Mary died at Annie's home, then granddad came to live with us in Portrack for a couple of years.

The End: *We never got any pocket money, I think Granddad had spent everything by then. I remember when he got the bus in Portrack where we lived, he used to up with his stick and run up the street, so that's how fit he was to go to the town to get his beer I suppose to the pubs and betting offices. He was a man of his time. My mother also looked after my dad who was an invalid, my dad, William Hart was only 48 when he died on the second of March 1952. I was 14 on the 17th March, St Patrick's Day the same year. Albert was about 92 when he died in a care home in Billingham in 1965.*

The Irish Sweepstake was set up in 1930 to fund Irish hospitals the sweep was one of the largest employers in Ireland with 4000 employees, mainly poorly paid women at one point with millions of tickets sold worldwide, a large proportion to the immigrant Irish community in the USA. For a while the government was delighted with the revenue but stakeholders grew wealthy at the expense of the prize to administration ratios and the hospitals received less and less. Eventually it is estimated that just 10% of the revenue actually made it to the hospitals due to the corrupt system. The Sweepstake was replaced by the Irish Lotto in 1987.

At Ashmores: one of the first prizes of £30,000 was won by a Golden Miller ticket holder Albert Hooten of Stockton who was Albert Sexton's workmate, he took the day off work to listen to the Grand National on the radio and never returned to his job as a bar straightener at Ashmores, retiring immediately. People who drew favourites often sold shares in their tickets and Albert Hooten sold a share to a commission agent from Hartlepool and a quarter share to his sister-in-law Isabel Braithwaite and a quarter share to Albert Sexton. However, another young workmate who was offered the share first hadn't come up with his money when the time came to send off the counterfoils to Ireland, so the share was offered to Albert.

.

The legendary Golden Miller, 1927-1957 won five Gold Cup races at Cheltenham and the 1934 Grand National by five lengths. A bronze statue to this magnificent horse now graces the courtyard at Cheltenham. It is said that the hooves are gradually being worn down by punters who touch them for luck.

The Corner of Francis Street and Queen Street c 1975. Thornaby's many betting shops were more social than gambling, as were Bingo Halls which began as social clubs. Below, the Mayfair.

Winifred's World

Contained in three neat handwritten exercise books Winifred Hope chronicled day to day life in Thornaby seen through the eyes of an ordinary young girl born in 1917. Daughter Sandra Briggs recognised the importance of her mother's work and has now gifted these valuable documents to Thornaby Archives for preservation. In this extract Winnie describes how she coped with a devastating childhood infection of polio.

Some time between 1923 and 1924 there was a polio epidemic. It was at this time that I had a severe attack of measles. On recovery from this, I was in a weak state and I was in direct line for the polio virus. I was ill for many weeks. I can remember the onset - pain in my limbs, feeling ill, diagnosed headachey. Mother called the doctor in and he diagnosed infantile paralysis, as it was called then. There was no known treatment and one lived or died. I was ill for many weeks, but with good nursing I recovered, but I was unable to walk. My right leg was useless. Mother spent day and night nursing me - hot cloths and rubbing with olive oil and when father came in from work he took over. I was well cared for and recovered the use of my leg, but was very ill. I was in bed for many months. My father used to wrap me in a blanket and swathe me round the back yard for fresh air. The nights were dark and he would tell me about the stars and point out the plough, the north star - the Great and Little Bears. I loved those walk a- bouts in the dark. I eventually recovered but I was lame in my right foot, and it caused my mother and father great sorrow. It was not until 1929 when Dr Crockett a doctor from the Yorkshire Children's Orthopaedic Hospital at Kirbymoorside examined me and decided something could be done to straighten my foot. I was admitted to the hospital in March 1930 and the operation was a success although it always remained a weak leg. Then the call came to go to the hospital for my operation. I went in March 1930. I did not return to school until Autumn 1931.

Winifred seen in her 90's. She passed away in 2014 aged 96.

Left: with her devoted father just a few years before her illness. John Hope had come from Birkenhead before the turn of the century and worked as a shipyard riveter, the family lived at 42 York Street.

Winifred's notebooks describe in detail her observations of life in a low income family in Thornaby between the wars from a woman's perspective. Running a home in working class Thornaby on a modest income was a challenge.

Vaccinations are now a routine part of growing up but Infantile Paralysis or Polio plagued Britain for nearly half a century. It was first identified in 1912 and when Winifred Hope caught the disease during the 1923 outbreak there was still no known cure.

Above: A polio victim in the USA with a wasted leg supported by callipers, Winifred endured a similar condition.

Right: The iron lung was developed in 1928 for patients whose lung muscles were paralysed so they could no longer breath unaided. Most patients only had to spend a short period in the iron lung before they regained the use of their lungs. But some patients with permanent paralysis of the lungs had to stay encased up to their necks in the large cumbersome contraptions for the rest of their lives.

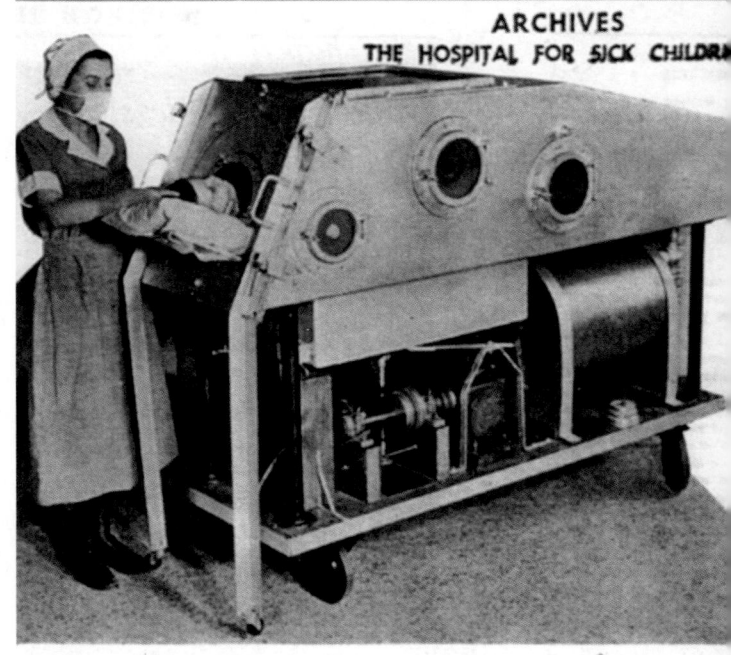

ARCHIVES
THE HOSPITAL FOR SICK CHILDREN

"IRON LUNGS" SAVE CHILDREN'S LIVES

One of the 28 "Iron Lungs" made at the Hospital for Sick Children, Toronto, for use in the infantile paralysis epidemic.

Winifred goes to the hospital

On receiving a communication from the Y. C. Orthopaedic Hospital I prepared to go to Kirbymoorside. I had to have an eye test and I had to be examined by the School Nurse who apologised for having to do so as she knew my head was clean and I was kept clean but "It was her duty" I was to travel with my mother to Northallerton Railway Station where I would be transported without mother to the hospital. On arriving at Northallerton the ambulance was waiting, it was a non-frightening car and in it there were several other children going to the hospital. It seemed a long journey, I remember going up Sutton Bank, I didn't know then that it was Sutton Bank, but I was glad when we reached the top. It was the first time I had been in a motor car. On arriving at the hospital I was amazed to see that the wards were open to the air. I can't remember what happened that day - I only know that clothes were taken away and wore as little as possible- just vest and knickers. After a few days settling in I was prepared to have my operation, after which I was in plaster and I was in bed for six weeks.

How kind everyone was. I was restless during the night for a while and nurse would bring me a mug of sweet tea. I would lie awake and watch the same stars we watched in the back yard in Thornaby. Great headlights would search the main road as they passed the hospital gates.

Winifred benefitted from the recently opened Yorkshire Orthopaedic Hospital for Crippled Children, which treated young people for polio and Tuberculosis. The photograph shows the open air treatment she describes, the boy at centre, his legs swathed in bandages and splints has had similar treatment.to Winifred.

The weeks passed and soon it was visiting day. A special bus left to pick up passengers at Thornaby and surrounding districts on the monthly visiting day to the hospital. It was lovely to see mother and father, and other members of the family. On one visiting day my Sunday School teacher travelled all the way on a motor bike. People were very kind and sent gifts and messages. They sent sweets and my favourite Clarnico marzipan bars, all kinds of fruit. These were all handed in, as were everyone else's gifts and were pooled and shared out among other patients either our own or someone else's.

After dinner every day we always received some sweets on visiting days, but the afternoon passed quickly and soon it was time to say goodbye. Most of us were sad when our parents went home, but we tried to cheer one another up.

Some of the children had been in the ward a long time and did not know when they were going home. Six weeks passed and one evening when all the girls who were mobile had gone for a walk in the fields with a nurse, Sister told me that she was going to take my plaster off. She cut it off with great shears then put my foot into a bath of warm water - what bliss. After settling me back into bed with a hot drink I waited for my friends to return from their walk. They soon noticed that my sling was no more and I know I would soon be up and joining them on their walks. Whilst I was in hospital we had lessons as usual and were encouraged to write. I joined the Whitby Gazette Children's Circle run by Uncle Ted. I wrote my first essay "Spring" and it was published. Someone at Thornaby who took the Whitby Gazette called at our house and said I had written an essay. and my name was in the paper. It caused quite a stir! I had many essays published and won three prizes. After having the plaster off I was soon up and about.

I loved the countryside, the wild flowers, bird life, beautiful trees and space- the hospital was set in beautiful surroundings. Time passed and in July I learned that I was to return home. It was sad to leave all my friends, nurses, sister and kind Dr. Crockett. I was taken by car to Northallerton where my father was waiting to take me home.

It was July 1930. I felt strange at home after the routine of hospital but it was a joyful occasion to be with my parents and brother & sisters. Mother looked after me devotedly so pleased that I could walk straight. It was the August Vacation at school so I expected to return in September - the new term. However, I was not allowed to go to school, but rested, I was kept under regular supervision of the surgeon from the hospital I had to practice exercises to strengthen my foot, but I improved week by week and became increasingly mobile.

The figures for 1947 showed that the summer epidemic was the worst since the disease was identified in 1912 with over 8000 cases nationwide. The disease continued to baffle the medical profession. Just like the common cold, only general advice and guidance could be given to the public. Local medical officers of health used their own discretion on preventative measures such as closing swimming baths and keeping children from places of entertainment to prevent the disease spreading.

It wasn't until 1952 that a vaccine was found in the USA and a mass vaccination programme began, later adopted in the UK.

Right: Elvis Presley is vaccinated on the Ed Sullivan TV Show in New York in 1956 before nearly 15 million viewers to help the government campaign.
Immunisation rates amongst American teenagers at the time were under 1%. Within six months of the live broadcast they had climbed to 80%.

Staindale Farm

A Farmer's Wife

Further extracts from Winifred Hope's remarkable journals: living in York Street, Winnie was called up for war work in 1944 to serve in the Women's Land Army. Posted twenty miles away near Great Smeaton she met Walter Horton another farm worker and they fell in love and eventually married. Winnie describes their lives as tenant farmers in Raisdale. A complete contrast to life in Thornaby: the next twenty years were marked by isolation, fatigue and cold.

Staindale farm was on the Western side of the valley so got very little sun. It had been unoccupied for years and had rising damp. Winnie later started teaching at Chop Gate, when daughter Sandra was seven although many of her farm duties remained. Winnie's experiences made her determined that Sandra would never become a farmer's wife.

The first weeks of settling in were difficult. Being springtime it was cold at 900 feet above sea level and there was hardly any heating in the house - We awoke to misty mornings, clouds rolled across the fields, one could see them swirling & curling along rolling mists & down below in Stokesley the sun would be shining.
My first work in the fields was planting potatoes. What an exhausting job. A half sack was tied around my waist and filled with potatoes. The seed potatoes were placed at sacks of strategic points in the furrows, so I could tell my apron when it was empty. What hard work - unused to farm labour and also being disabled I found it a daunting task but it had to be done - it was expected - a farmer's wife had to be able to work up and down the rows I went wondering how I had managed to drag myself along- but rest comes. I was allowed to go to the house to fix something to eat + no cooking to day. I had to see to the baby & make sandwiches then it was out to the fields again. If I was thankful when that task was done. I was utterly weary. The next outdoor job was hoeing turnips. I found I was not able to walk on the uneven ground, so I had a hand hoe & I had to kneel and hoe a few yards then end of it was drag my kneeling sack along and do another few yards and I did that until the turnips were done It was harder than potatoes. up & down -up and down. If I could have walked and hold it would have been easier but my foot and leg could not take the strain.

During the summer of 1945 we had been keeping a pig so that we would have a supply of meat for winter. The first winter, 1945-46 was dreadful - very little coal - very little money - one fire. During the wet weather I had to sit up at night and dry Walt's work clothes for next day. They had to be turned & heavy overcoats took a lot of drying out. Paraffin was always in short supply - we kept some on hand in case we were snowed in. Oil lamps were our only source of lighting. I used to mend clothes by the light of the fire.

"Walter cutting the corn. The sheaves are stooked, taken to the stackyard ready to be threshed at some point in the future. You are left with straw stack and sacks of grain in your granary" Sandra Briggs, daughter.

Threshing

Farmers helped each other as the thresher went from farm to farm. It was the old steam thresher in those days. Everyone hoped for a fine day & the farmer's wife had to take a cooked dinner, prepare tea for men. She usually had friends or relatives to help. First there was ten o'clocks. Baskets of scones, cakes, pies, sausage rolls, sandwiches & a huge can of tea would be taken to the stack yard where the men would enjoy the break, wash the dust down I have a chat. Then the engine would start and work proceeded until dinner time.

In the meantime pans of potatoes and vegetables would be cooking, perhaps steak & Kidney pie or a roast of beef, followed by pudding - steamed or apple pie with custard and more tea. Table was based in the farmhouse kitchen. At 1 o'clock work began until 3 pm when the ritual of 10 o clock would be repeated. Men worked until they finished or until five, when they came into the farmhouse for a sit-down tea. There was much baking done for threshing day - loads of washing up- but we were thankful when it was over and grateful to all the men who had come to help.

The farmhouse

I was managing to get some sort of order, I distempered the bedroom walls I gave the doors, windows a coat of paint, but it was all very bare & basic. There was nothing pretty - no carpet just clinically clean. Floors were scrubbed & just a rug on the floor. In due course a bath was installed in the back bedroom & this was indeed a luxury? This was years later. After bathing in a tin bath in front of the fire we hadn't a tin bath at first - we just washed ourselves down & of course Sandra had a baby bath. I was tired of this & I had £25 in the bank so I drew it out and bought a bath, a play pen and a supply of baby food as Sandra needed a more varied diet, and new clothes for her - winter was coming.

A black eye

One night before checking Walt had milked the cows it was very late and dark so I went out to round them up to bring them in for milking - and I had to go to the fields to find them. I took the dogs and as I was following them across the moor, there was an opening in a stone wall. Not knowing there was barbed wire across I went through it as a short cut but found myself hanging on the barbed wire by the flesh underneath my eye. I could not get the hooked wire worked out of my eye- I was utterly helpless. I had to pull & tear the skin to free myself. What a terrible painful eye, blood everywhere. I should have been to the hospital to have it stitched, but there was no one to take me and no time to spare. I was in agony on threshing day with the heat of the oven and all the activity. It took months to heal.

Bonnie the pony with Sandra, left.

Right: Staindale Farm. "Seeing the lights on in the farmhouse is still the best sight in the world" Sandra Briggs

Walter Horton cutting corn with a binder on his David Brown tractor

My weak foot

Sandra was growing up and it was a lonely life for her and also for me. We went for months without seeing or speaking to anyone except the postman. I had to do the daily chores and now try to manage some time in the day to play with her. Also to read to her and teach her to speak properly. She was a patient child, she played happily by herself when I was busy – which was always. I could now take her with me to the fields when I was expected to work. At this time I was experiencing trouble with my foot. Walking on rough land as I worked in the fields had not helped- my weak foot became weaker. I used to suffer intense pain. The broken toe did not help either. I found it difficult to bend my toes and I developed a stamping gait.

Winter 1947

Sowing time, harvest, and threshing – preserve making passed and it was Sandra's 2nd Birthday. It was the same routine – nothing changed except the weather.
On Boxing Day we were going to Thornaby to visit my parents and have dinner at my sister's house. There had been several falls of snow in the time heading up to Christmas, and there was a light cover on this Boxing Day. After the farm chores, we set off in the car about mid- day . As we drove down Carlton Bank the car went out to control- under the snow was ice and the car started to slide sideways. There is a deep ghyll on Carlton Bank Top and this is where it happened. How Walt controlled the car, we will never know. God was with us that day. I prayed as I had never prayed before. The wheels could not grip and we really thought it was the end. The road was narrow and the ghyll just a few feet away. It only lasted a few seconds but felt like an eternity. At last Walt steered to safer ground and we breathed a sigh of relief. We eventually landed at our destination – we had a lovely afternoon and too soon it was time to say goodbye. This time we went back up Clay Bank.

Snowed in

When we reached home it was all hands on deck, fastening hen houses, making gruel for calves, Walt milking – getting Sandra to bed, feeding the stock- by 10 o clock we were exhausted. Then the snow came. We were literally fastened in. When we opened the back door we were faced with a wall of

snow. We had to dig our way out- the back kitchen was flooded as the snow fell in. With great effort we reached the cow byres as the cows were overdue for milking and there was a lot of moo- ing going on . There was no chance of getting the milk to the end of the road- we would have to dig out and we had to dig for ¼ mile so we made little progress that day. Snow fell relentlessly for days. Walt and I would to clear a way to the road for the tractor – we worked during then night. Only to find it filled in with drifted snow. Sometimes it was filled in as we dug- hopeless. The ghylls were level with snow, stone walls and tree tops could not be seen, the ground was level with snow- we were just in a white world.

We were worried about the sheep. Walt went out on foot with the dogs to bring them nearer the house. I went sometimes with him at night and we searched with lanterns. The dogs found them and we dug them out. You could tell where they were because there were holes in the snow where they were breathing even though their bodies were covered.

Winter on Staindale Farm

The road from Chop Gate to Carlton was blocked and the milk wagon could not get through. Eventually the farmers dug out the road to CG piling the snow at each side like walls and taking the milk for collection to C.G. by tractor. Farms on the roadside were not so badly placed but such as we who were set back had to keep a road open to first get to the main road. For weeks we worked and dug until early morning. It was a round of digging, feeding stock, making hot meals and drying clothes. Sandra and I were never out or saw anyone from Boxing Day 1946 to Good Friday 1947. What a winter! However, spring came at last as we, as well as other farmers were weary.

On Good Friday, Sandra and I went to stay with my parents at Thornaby. We had not seen anyone to talk to except the postman since Boxing Day. We had been isolated for 3 months. Walt had taken the tenancy in the first place for 3 years, so I was looking forward to leaving before Sandra went to school. She needed to get used to being with her peers. I had put up with such a lot of loneliness and inconvenience and was hoping to be in civilisation again.

Walt renews the tenancy

After another snowy, freezing winter of 1947-1948 our three years were over and we awaited the arrival of the agent in early spring. I was looking forward to leaving for another tenancy. Sandra would soon be going to school and she needed to get used to children her own age- she had lived as well as I – a lonely life for 3 years. The day for the agent's visit arrived. I didn't know what had taken place, but I was not prepared for the news that Walt had signed a new tenancy agreement. The bottom fell out of my world. I was disabled, I had struggled for 3 years in isolated conditions, had no friends, a damp house, this was the last straw.

It was worse for Sandra. She had never played with another child - she needed friends, just as I needed friends. If I had had any money or anywhere to go- I would have left. But there was nowhere. My parents were old I could not afford to keep Sandra and me I'm sure would have felt it wrong to encourage me - I was married and that was it.

Winnie 1964

In 1952 Winnie became a local teacher and practiced until her retirement, she was highly respected. Walter gave up Staindale farm after 20 years and went to work on other farms. The farm had been a huge burden on the couple and their daughter Sandra remembers them being financially better off afterwards. Ironically Walter returned to work at the farm where they had met during the war. Winnie taught at nearby Great Smeaton School.
"I remember the farm on sale day, watching our animals being taken away just about broke my heart." Says Sandra.

Winnie and Walter 1970

A grateful thanks to Sandra Briggs for her help in preparing this feature on her mother's journals.

Before they Disappeared

The 1970's said goodbye to many of Thornaby's Victorian industrial streets, most had seen a century of use, probably far longer than the builders and developers ever dreamt of at the time. Our portfolio contains scans made from recently discovered negatives recording the dying moments of some popular streets. We can only begin to imagine the epic stories some of these buildings could tell us.

Top: Anderson Street before demolition, one could not wish for a more "corner" corner shop, this is at the intersection of Teesdale Street in about 1976. To the left of the shop one of several nearby workshops where artisans and tradespeople performed a host of skilled tasks, downstairs was often a stable for a horse and cart. This photograph demonstrates how rudimentary houses were in industrial Thornaby: flattened porticos; no ornamentation and in the case of these streets, no bay windows, these were probably two bedroom. Most were well crafted though and they stood the test of time.

Left: Summer 1976, the JCB has just laid bare the basic construction of this typical kitchen: a thin slate roof, a single plastered wall which would have done little to keep the damp or cold out. The larder kept food cool in summer.

Above: Grants garage on Thornaby Road before closure. **Below:** the Queens Cinema, Mandale Road, demolition is under way in 1977. The stained-glass windows lit the eastern staircase. Beyond, rows of shops have now gone, opening up a new vista onto George Street and Barnard Street which are also soon to disappear ready for the construction of the A66 dual carriageway.

Top left: Cleveland View on Mandale Road began life as a fine dwelling with superb views across the wilderness to Middlesbrough. William Strikes appear to have established one of their many garden centres there later until the 1930's when Bob Alexander motors moved in and ran their business as The Harewood Garage. Alexanders later moved to Trafalgar Street. A substantial electric sign: " STRIKES FOR SEEDS" at the back of the house was a distinctive feature of the Thornaby landscape, visible on journeys to Thornaby from Middlesbrough. The sign remained until the building was demolished soon after this photograph was taken in 1975. Just visible in the far distance "The Torch" a water tower at Cork Insulation and Asbestos, near Thornaby station another landmark soon to go.

Charles Ingle, Thornaby's main printer and bookbinder set up shop at 58 Mandale Road at about the turn of the 20th century after moving from Denton in Lincolnshire. Son Vince Ingle later took on the business. Charles Ingle established a reliable outfit supplying most of the local print demands. The Head Wrightson's in house magazine was a good example "The Right Ahead" was key bread and butter work as was the Thornaby Town Council Minutes. All demanded forensic detailed type setting and proofreading. The shop's crème façade remained in the same style throughout it's life.

Far left: Thornaby Station in 1975 showing original timber infrastructure probably unchanged since 1882 when it was opened. The station still evokes a range of emotions for Thornaby people and once there was probably no one in the town who hadn't encountered it's sweeping platforms over the years.

Above: number 14 Harewood Place before demolition. Cleveland View is in the background.

Above: Hartington Street and Charles Street 1977 await demolition. The woman in foreground is identified as Ivy Logan on her way back to Cuthbert Street. A Facebook posting brought many affectionate memories of the street, families mentioned include: the Hezzeltines, Honneysetts, McCues, Sayers, Butlers, Pinnegars and Walkers. Ken Birch ran the shop until it's last days after the Beatties who moved out in the early 1960's.

Jacky and Esther Brown who lived at the end house, enjoy a summer afternoon at the other end of Hartington Street possibly a year earlier.

Right: and this is the fate that awaits most of our subjects.

Left: back lane between Hartington Street and Cuthbert Street, 1974.

MERRY XMAS 1936.

Outside Batty's pub, Hope Street. Jim Danks back row second from right. Thirty years later Jim would buy the freeholds of the empty surrounding streets to develop his haulage business and scrapyard.

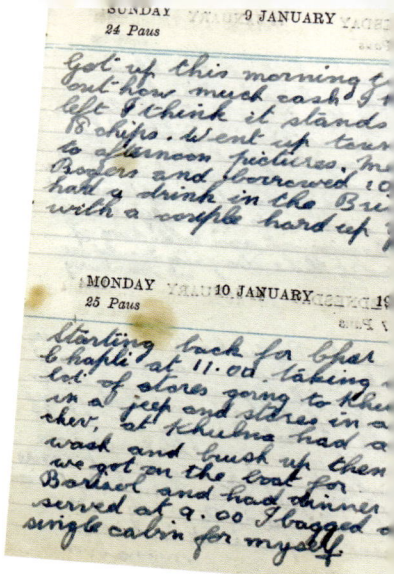

Jimmy Danks: Far East Diary

When the 18 year old Jim Danks enlisted in the Royal Air Force Volunteer Reserve in September 1941 he could never have imagined the momentous events that lay ahead. Jim would play his part in the turning point of the whole war when the Japanese were finally routed in Burma in June 1944. He spent three whole years in India and Burma without leave, driving and maintaining RAF vehicles and guarding secret airfields. He witnessed the effects of the 1943 cyclone that had devastated land and crops. Three million people had died in the 1943 Bengal famine. Even in the services food was continually scarce.

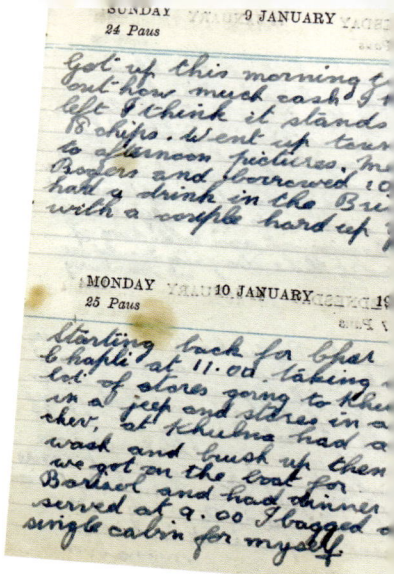

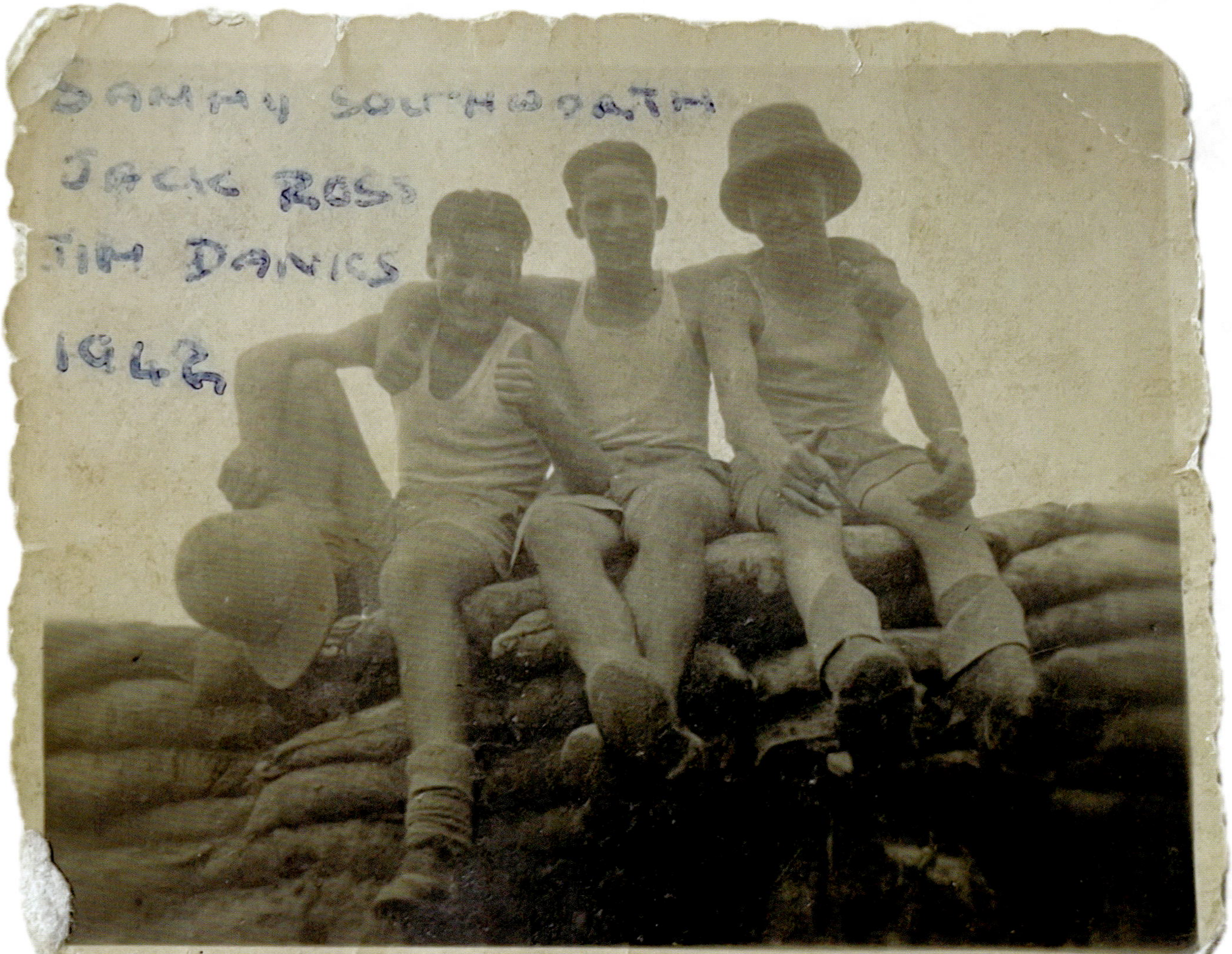

Yet the Far East campaign was sidelined and resources absorbed by the other war fronts until 1944. Jim seems to have spent long stretches waiting for orders or travelling vast distances across difficult terrain to carry them out. Jim like many of his fellow servicemen suffered malaria, the effects of cold, heat, monsoon rain, and starvation.

The 1944 Diary: extracts

THURSDAY 3rd February
Went to Chabatia today by country boat bought some stores at the market. It was hard going I paddled all the way back about 15 miles. Had a bad scare at about midnight a tiger was on the prowl just outside my tent.

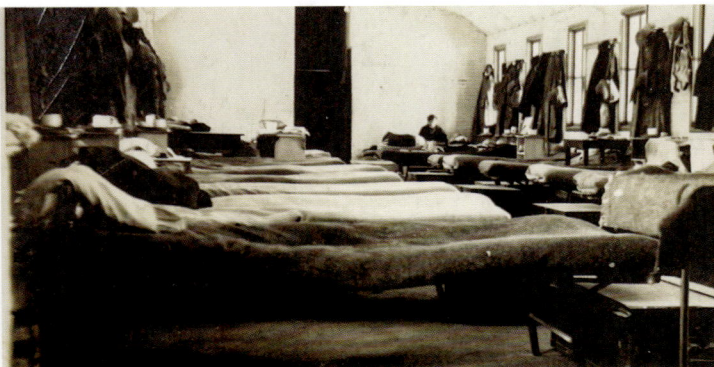

WEDNESDAY 1st March
Bit of a flap on at Tiffin (lunch) time enemy aircraft reported two miles away and no gunners to be found nothing happened thank god.

FRIDAY 31st March
Took my first lesson on driving a waggon. Made a good effort but still need plenty of practice.
Like many other service people Jim gained skills in the RAF. He learned how to drive, repair and overhaul heavy goods vehicles which would benefit him after the war.

SATURDAY 20th May
I am rather lucky I have just been informed that my old squadron has had it proper at ————— It is two years since I came to India.

Top: RAF on the town, Calcutta c1943, Jim far right.
Above: One of the many billets. Some were more basic.
Left: With aircrew c1943

MONDAY 26th June
Still raining everywhere is flooded everything is wet. Oh boy what a country.

SATURDAY 23rd September
Pulled in beside a down train full of my old mates. There were all loaded down with old Jap rifles etc. that they got at Palel

Nearly 60,000 Japanese had died, mainly in the fierce battles of Imphal and Kohima from March until June 1944, their air supplies were cut off and they were left abandoned and starving.   By mid 1944 Allied air forces enjoyed air supremacy over Burma and India.

SUNDAY 24th September
This traveling is a bind and it is getting me down.

MONDAY 25th September
Passed straight through Cal today we are now heading away from it.
Passed an ambulance train full of Japs, what a state they were in.

At Kohima a force of only 1,500 Allied troops faced 15,000 Japanese in fierce battles but by June the Japanese had been defeated.

TUESDAY 26th September
Pulled into the last station this morning. Waited all day for a boat. We still do not know where we are going yet.

TUESDAY 10th October
We had a horrible time today travelling on the back of a waggon is no fun on these roads. It was a longer journey than I thought and we spent the night in a rest camp. When we passed through Kohima there was still signs of the heavy fighting that was there.

WEDNESDAY 11th October
Finished the last part of the journey today. Received two letters which cheered me up no end. And then we were told that we shall have to do that road journey again tomorrow and go to Agatala for a course on Armoured cars this means another three days travelling at least. We are now in Palel

Communications between service personnel and the home front were difficult but were crucial to moral, after being cut off for years. Letters if they arrived and weren't lost at sea to Japanese attacks, took a long time to get through especially during Jim's early years in India.

WEDNESDAY 18th October
We are still in the rest camp. And we are in Manipur the place the Japs were after. It is a long time since I had a square meal and I guess it will be a long time before I see one again.

Food was scarce, local rice production badly affected by the 1943 cyclone and the Japanese occupation of Burma.

MONDAY 27th November
Up again this morning at 5.30 because we have a long run this time. Reached Dimapur about 6.00 in the evening and went into the rest camp for the night for some badly needed sleep. This job is not hard but the mental strain is terrific.

SUNDAY 3 December
Started off this morning and crossed the border into Burma. Travelling through country strewn with graves and ruined materials. Camped by the roadside for the night.

WEDNESDAY 6th December
Piled our kit on to two 3 ton wagons and started off for our own camp which is not so far behind the front line. Most of the way was a nasty smell of rotting bodies. We now have to carry our guns everywhere because of stray Japs and snipers which are plentiful. Received a lot of mail.

The 1944 battles of Imphal and Kohima changed the entire course of the war when the occupying Japanese were driven out of Burma thanks to the allies' air superiority. Jim played his part, although in 1944 he seems to have been involved in vital but routine air support rather than direct conflict.

Mary Danks was shocked to receive this studio portrait of her undernourished son through the post, it was taken in 1943 in Calcutta.

MONDAY 25th December
Woke up this morning with a head like six I was very drunk last night mainly due to the pilots we were with, they drink like fishes. I drank a ½ pint of rum ½ pint of gin and three pints of beer. No more for me for a while.

SATURDAY 30th December
Still hanging on to dear life. Things are still shaky and dizzy. Five us were in the dock with malaria there is only four now Paddy a corporal passed away this morning.

At least 15,000 British and Indian soldiers died in the campaign. Three quarters of all losses were caused by Malaria, dysentery or dengue fever. Heat stroke also claimed many lives. Jim continued to suffer from malaria intermittently until he was in his mid 60's.

SUNDAY 31st December
Well here we are the end of the book and the year thank god. It has had its ups and downs. The last day passed quite nicely fever gone.

Left: Burning mustard gas canisters on Bowes Moor January 1947. Many were also buried on the moor.

Jim returned home from the heat of the tropics in 1947 but further extremes awaited him before he was demobbed. He was despatched to Bowes Moor to the national chemical warfare agent site which now presented the government with huge disposal problems. Jim was part of a team put to work to dispose of huge quantities of mustard gas canisters during one of the worst winters on record, in 1947.

Huts similar to those on Bassleton Lane 1946

Bassleton Lane

The camp

Aerial view 1946

Homes for Heroes ?

Jim had taken dancing lessons in India and had become a popular partner. He met another good dancer Joyce whom he called Sue and married in October 1947. Their first son Terry was born in a one room flat above a chip shop.

The Danks' next home was a Nissen hut locally known as the squatters' huts, on Bassleton Lane. In August 1946, tens of thousands of people, mainly ex-servicemen and their families, like the Danks moved into empty military camps around Britain as squatters. It was a reaction to the housing crisis and over the course of the occupations, more than 45,000 people were involved in the takeover of most of the military camps in Britain. Few homes had been built during the war and many had been damaged or destroyed in bombing raids. This act of major civil disobedience was supported by the general public who sympathised with so many who had contributed to the war effort and now found themselves homeless. Jim and his partner Joyce along with other servicemen took over one of a series of 18 servicemen's huts on Bassleton Lane that had been abandoned at the close of the war. The couple soon turned it into a comfortable living space.

However during the Christmas of 1949 they faced eviction while Sue was pregnant with Christine, their second child. When it went to court the judge commended Jim as a thoroughly decent young man who had hit upon hard times. He regretted that although he had to follow the letter of the law, he would allow them to stay until after the birth.

With the help of his brother Judd, Jim bought a lorry to begin his own haulage business. When ships were in dock he would work round the clock for weeks. By 1964 Jim had a fleet of eleven vehicles.

Jim will probably be best remembered for the scrap yard in Wedgewood Street and Queen Street West off Thornaby Road he ran for many years with the help of his sons. The Yard was compulsory purchased to make way for the A66.

Left: The Queen Street West Garages c1966

Jim's 1939/45 Star, Burma Star, Defence Medal and War Medal

Right : Jim c1995, took his medals with him on a Rhine cruise that coincided with the 50th anniversary of Victory in Europe day. He intrigued the other guests and locals that night by proudly wearing his medals at dinner.

We are grateful to Jim's daughter Mary Danks for her help in preparing this feature.

Alvira Costello: When the Nazis came for us
Isola-del-Lire 1943

A lot of Germans occupied our village, we were just a country village, with horses and carts no cars then. We were not very far from Monte Cassino so I could see the fire going all night, the bombs dropping and whatever at the big battle of Monte Cassino, I knew nothing about the war but then saw all the flashing lights in the distance, I was only 15 or 16 during this time. We were a big family, there was ten of us, then my uncle lived with us and my brother got married and his children lived at our house, so there was 15 of us altogether. We had to evacuate our village, we had to get out of the house and the Germans occupied our place. In the bedrooms they kept their horses. We couldn't go back to our own place for months, we went to a house in the middle of the country far away from us.

One night there was me, my mam and my two sisters who were pregnant, they were all living together crammed on top of each other in two bedrooms. The German SS came and they chased us all over and said they were going to take us to peel the potatoes for the troops but my mother God Bless her soul said no because they'll be taken to the brothel as comfort women for the soldiers. When we were outside at night, it was only moonlight, the German pointed his gun at my mother's head and told her if we ran away they were going to shoot her. Me mam said "Run, run, run for your lives "There was an Austrian who could speak Italian and he said "Run like hell." I ran away from home, we were hiding at a friend's house for three weeks but first hid in the countryside for days, we were starving.

The Germans used to take the men for digging and the women for the brothels. They took all our food, we had to bury what we could in containers along with some clothing because they'd take everything you had, even bedding. What they couldn't take they destroyed, they couldn't carry all our barrels of wine so they stuck their bayonets through the wood and all the wine leaked out into the road. We went through hell in the war, although we were better off than some because we worked on the land and we could hide a bit of food eventually. Then their planes came and dive bombed us. Me and my sister used to lay down in a ditch for cover. When the Germans left we went back to our houses and they had used the bedrooms as stables for the horses and we had to clear it all out, then we were all ill with malaria. We were practically dying, no medicine or doctors, until the Americans arrived after about a month and they brought tablets, they used to give us quinine tablets. Everything is marvellous in Italy now, everyone has a car but then we were starving. The Germans took everything, they didn't even leave you with a blanket.

In 1946 Alvira was offered work in Thornaby by the Paleschi family in Westbury Street through a relative in nearby Sora where they had originated from. She later married and settled in Gilmour Street, living in Thornaby for the rest of her life.

Film still from "Rome Open City" 1945

A grateful thanks to all those who contributed to this project including:

Dr. Julia Routh
Sarah Booth
Morwenn Breare
Raymond Todd
Ken Payne
Eileen Dobson
Stephen Dobson
Ann Peterson
Nancy Skelton

Fred Costello
Dorothy Toulson
Winnie McHugh
Jerrod Henry
Stuart Bell
David Allport
Mary Danks
Pamela Danks
Kath Crossan

Angela Costello
Josie Godwin
Lillian Watts
Tony Bartley
Cath Harrison
Ian Murray
Jack Green
Frank Mallon
Ann Wilson

Audrey Henderson
Karen Bibbings
Sandra Briggs
Lesley Palmer
Alison Poole
John Watton
Marilyn Proctor
Peter Costello